The Power of the WARSHIPS

The B-B 'Warships' of Classes 42 and 43 were arguably the most underrated Type 4 locomotives on the British Railways (BR) network. The average annual mileage of the Class 42s was 95,000 and the Class 43s 80,000, compared with 69,000 for Class 47s, 65,000 for Class 52s and 57,000 for Class 45s. The power-to-weight ratio of the B-B locomotives was impressive, over 2,200hp being developed in a locomotive weighing just over 78 tons. Accelerating through Sydney Gardens at Bath with the 10.45SuO Taunton–Paddington of 2 May 1965 is No D860 *Victorious. Brian Stephenson*

Title page (below):
The design of the 'Warships' was based on German railway-engineering principles, using expertise gained over many years of operating locomotives with high-speed diesel engines coupled to hydraulic transmissions. The Western Region (WR) initiative of using tried and tested designs (with modifications) made sense compared with the British Transport Commission (BTC) approach of running a pilot scheme, which resulted in a large number of poorly designed and unreliable diesel-electric locomotives from a variety of companies working on the BR system. Heading a 13-coach 'Cornish Riviera Express' past Dawlish Warren on Sunday 25 June 1961 is No D868 *Zephyr. M. Pope*

Title page (right):
This picture shows the standard style of 'Warship' nameplate as fitted to Class 42 No 818 *Glory*. When the final 'Warships' were withdrawn in 1972 there was outrage at the £50 price tag being demanded by BR for the aluminium nameplates. In 2005 £5,000 would not be sufficient at auction to buy a 'Warship' nameplate in good condition! *John Vaughan*

The Power of the
WARSHIPS

John Vaughan

OPC
An imprint of
Ian Allan Publishing

Contents

First published 2005

ISBN 0 86093 590 6

© Ian Allan Publishing Ltd 2005

Published by Oxford Publishing Co

an imprint of Ian Allan Publishing Ltd, Hersham, Surrey KT12 4RG.
Printed by Ian Allan Printing Ltd, Hersham, Surrey KT12 4RG.

Code: 0508/

Visit the Ian Allan Publishing website at www.ianallanpublishing.co.uk

Introduction

In the case of every other book in the Oxford Publishing Co 'Power' series a single locomotive type or class, including any sub-classes, is featured. However, the term 'Warship' includes a diverse range of locomotives that were introduced in the late 1950s and early 1960s, all with high-speed diesel engines, hydraulic transmissions, names with (mostly) naval implications and above all else a significant German influence. They were to be the product of the North British Locomotive Co (NBL) and BR's Swindon Works and in later years would be referred to as Classes 41, 42 and 43. (It should perhaps be noted that a later attempt (in 1980) to apply the collective name 'Warships' to English Electric Class 50 diesel-electric locomotives failed to be adopted by either the public at large or the modern-traction enthusiast fraternity.)

Although the pre-Nationalisation Southern Railway and London, Midland & Scottish Railway companies had tinkered with main-line diesel traction it was not until the British Transport Commission (BTC) produced its comprehensive Modernisation Plan in March 1955 that a new traction policy emerged. Initially some £150 million was allocated to the procurement of diesel locomotives — a staggering sum 50 years ago. Long-term plans envisaged a fleet of 2,500 diesel locomotives, but before this took place a Pilot Scheme was announced. The BTC wanted to evaluate various types of diesel locomotive in different power ranges from a number of manufacturers, which was more of a political decision than a practical one. After World War 2 British industry was in a run-down state and companies (and voters) were looking to the Government for support. Unemployment was also a factor in influencing decisions as to how the workshops of Britain could be kept busy. A more sensible and cost-effective strategy than buying British would have been for the BTC to take advantage of the experience gained in other countries that had implemented a diesel-traction policy decades before BR. In particular the United States of America had huge expertise of diesel-electric locomotives, while West Germany had made enormous advances in the field of diesel-hydraulic traction. Japan also had experience in the field, but, with World War 2 having finished only a decade before, one can imagine the outcry that would have ensued had large orders for BR locomotives been placed abroad while British factories stood idle!

In the mid-1950s the various regions still had a modicum of autonomy, even though the BTC ultimately controlled national policy. The BTC recognised that any evaluation should include some diesel-hydraulic machinery, and it was commonly known that the Western Region (WR) was enthusiastic about that prospect. To simplify a long story, arrangements were made whereby the component parts for German high-speed diesel engines and hydraulic transmissions were sent to the UK for assembly in British workshops, in this case by the North British Locomotive Co and BR's own workshops at Swindon (and their respective sub-contractors).

However, the WR was not given a totally free hand, and, while the WR CME was taking all necessary actions to design a lightweight 78-ton B-B (*i.e.* with two four-wheeled bogies)

2,200hp locomotive, the BTC had ordered on 16 November 1955 from NBL five large 117-ton diesel-hydraulics using two 1,000hp MAN engines with Voith transmissions. The locomotives were substantially built, on diesel-electric principles far removed from the WR's optimum requirements.

In the meantime the WR had authority to order three 78-ton 2,200hp diesel-hydraulics, which were to be built by BR's Swindon Works, the order being placed in January 1956. The locomotives would have German Maybach engines and Mekydro transmissions and be based closely on the German 'V200' diesel-hydraulic design. One of the problems encountered was fitting the engines, transmissions, fuel tanks, train-heating boilers and many other components into a locomotive that was required to fit the smaller dimensions of the BR loading gauge. Although the goal was ultimately achieved, many tens of thousands of drawing-room hours were spent trying to accommodate the various components. This was achieved partly by a novel form of construction whereby the basic frame tubes, longitudinals, cross braces, body sides and panelling were virtually all load-bearing and therefore 'stressed'. Before the three B-B locomotives were completed an order for a further 30 similar (but not identical) locomotives was placed, all to be built at Swindon Works.

It is worth mentioning that on 16 November 1955 NBL had also secured an order for six small 1,000hp B-B diesel-hydraulic locomotives, using German MAN engines and Voith transmissions, for use on the WR. This was followed by an order on 5 November 1957 for a further 52 locomotives but with engines uprated to 1,100hp. (Many enthusiasts called these locomotives 'Baby Warships', and they would later become known officially as Class 22s.) This was quickly followed by an order on 3 July 1958 for 33 B-B diesel-hydraulics, this time to be built at NBL's Glasgow works and featuring German MAN engines and Voith transmission (all built under licence by NBL). These 2,200hp locomotives had what were in effect two of the same MAN L12V18/21B diesel engines that were fitted to the small 1,100hp locomotives mentioned above.

In April 1959 a final order was placed for five more 78-ton Swindon locomotives.

The BTC had intended that, initially, diesel locomotives should be introduced to specific areas, and as part of this plan

Above:
The original 117-ton A1A-A1A 'Warships' (later known retrospectively as Class 41s) were not welcomed by the WR. It was at the insistence of the BTC that the first main-line diesel-hydraulic locomotives utilised heavy-engineering principles historically associated with diesel-electric machinery with large, slow-speed diesel engines. Five locomotives of the type were constructed by the North British Locomotive Co (NBL) at its Queen's Park works in Glasgow. The locomotives each cost £87,500, but that cost did not fully reflect all the drawing-office work undertaken or parts (such as the buffers) provided free of charge; the true cost would have run into six figures. This view shows No D600 *Active* in ex-works condition.

it announced its intention to 'dieselise' as soon as possible all services west of Newton Abbot, calculating that just 130 diesel locomotives could operate all traffic in the area. When the new diesel-hydraulics for the WR were delivered to Swindon from NBL Glasgow they were soon out on test, not only to acquire operational data but also to familiarise train crews and technicians with the new machinery. The first of the original A1A-A1A 'Warships', No D600, arrived on the WR in January 1958, the second, No D601, entering traffic in March 1958. Before the third locomotive appeared the first lightweight B-B, No D800, emerged from Swindon and entered traffic on 11 August 1958. The last of the five 117-ton 'Warships' was delivered on 20 January 1959; between 7 November 1958 and 25 October 1961 37 more B-Bs were built at Swindon, and between 6 July 1960 and 28-June 1962 33 arrived from NBL in Scotland.

In terms of æsthetics the appearance of the 'Warships' was controversial. The origins of the B-B were in the German 'V200' class, but they were not overly similar. They were distinctive, with clean lines, and they were certainly better-looking than some of the later classes of diesel-electric locomotive that had large headcode boxes at roof level.

The A1A-A1A locomotives carried their length well and were spoiled only by the ugly headcode boxes that appeared in their later years. All locomotives emerged from works in green livery with a narrow white band along the bodyside, a later embellishment being small yellow warning panels on the cab ends. The next livery applied was maroon, but that was relatively short-lived because in 1967 BR adopted all-over blue with full yellow cab ends as its standard livery. There were a number of detailed differences in liveries (in terms of panel size, for example), and some locomotives never received the maroon livery. Others, such as No D800 and D601, were withdrawn while still in green livery. The positions of numbers and BR 'arrows' logo also varied, and most permutations are illustrated within the pages of this book.

All of the original 2,000hp locomotives and, with a couple of exceptions, the later 2,200hp locomotives were named after past or contemporary Royal Navy vessels, and consequently all 76 locomotives, with either four- or six-wheeled bogies, became known as as 'Warships'. No D600 *Active* was the first diesel locomotive in BR ownership to be named. (A full list of the names is supplied in the 'Factfile' on pages 110 and 111.)

By mid-1958 the early 'Warships' were working crack express trains between Paddington and Plymouth and Penzance and between Paddington, Bristol and Weston-super-Mare. The old steam depots were ill equipped to maintain the new diesels, and any serious problems resulted in a locomotive's being hauled to Swindon Works for rectification. However, gradually new facilities at Plymouth (Laira), Newton Abbot, Bristol Bath Road, Old Oak Common, Cardiff Canton, Swansea (Landore) and, later, Newport (Ebbw Junction) came on stream, and the diesels were given the attention they deserved. In the early days there was frequently steam/diesel double-heading, particularly over the South Devon banks, but gradually the 'Warships' (and the 'Baby Warships') made inroads into the legions of WR 4-6-0 steam locomotives on main-line services.

As might be expected there were many faults with the new motive power, but with the original two 'Warships' covering over 150,000 miles by 1960 the overall picture was encouraging. However, the other three fared less well — a fact that, sadly, was attributable to poor-quality British-made components in those particular machines. Within a year or two the type was displaced on Class 1 trains east of Plymouth by the lighter and more powerful B-B 'Warships', and with lower-mileage rosters (combined with lengthy idle periods, while spares were obtained from NBL) annual mileages settled down to between 55,000 and 70,000 miles. The five locomotives spent their entire lives based on Plymouth Laira depot save for a short time in 1967, just before their demise, when they were transferred to Swansea Landore to haul coal trains in the area.

The lightweight B-B 'Warships' revolutionised WR main-line services. Although initially diagrammed on expresses between London and Bristol and the West Country, as time went by they inevitably worked inter-regional expresses that ran on a northeast/northwest–southwest axis. It should be mentioned that, although in 1962 the 'Warships' were mostly in charge of Paddington–Bristol Temple Meads trains, the new 1,700hp 'Hymek' (later Class 35) diesel-hydraulics had a monopoly on Paddington–South Wales trains, and from the same year 'Western' (Class 52) diesel-hydraulics shared many of these Class 1 duties.

In the late 1950s the B-B 'Warships' worked to Wolverhampton Low Level and Birkenhead, and from 1962 they could often be found on the old North & West road between Newport, Hereford, Shrewsbury and Crewe. They also had stints on the Birmingham Direct line, between Paddington and the UK's second city, and from time to time worked services between Paddington and Worcester/Hereford via Oxford. Swindon-built examples took over the Waterloo–Exeter services in September 1964 and would be associated with the line for seven years. Generally speaking the B-B 'Warships' could be found anywhere from Paddington to Penzance (including Torbay), from Penzance to Birmingham and from Newport and Bristol to Paddington. Miscellaneous workings were almost infinite within the WR — by way of a non-exhaustive example Exeter–Barnstaple/Ilfracombe trains, Bristol–Weymouth workings, holiday trains on branch lines such as that to Newquay and occasionally in the Golden Valley between Swindon and Gloucester. Special trains, excursions and Royal Train workings took the class to many obscure corners of the network. In the eyes of many their halcyon days were in 1968/9, when selected Class 42s double-headed the most prestigious West Country expresses at record-breaking speeds on an upgraded timetable.

As time went on the 'Warships' were displaced from some Class 1 and 2 passenger workings and appeared more frequently on freight trains. Such workings were many and varied, and the best summary is provided by the photographs and captions that follow, the B-B diesel-hydraulics being shown hauling engineering trains, vans, coal, china clay, cement, stone and ballast, automobiles, fertiliser, milk and mixed freight trains.

During the course of their careers the 'Warships' were afflicted by a range of technical problems. On many occasions fragments of metal in the lubricating oil or on filters provided evidence of a breakdown of moving parts within. The Maybach engine was superior to the NBL/MAN example, accounting for only 2.5% of failures on Swindon-built machines. Although the engine had a propensity to crack cylinder heads, this was not a fault of the engine *per se* but the result of a lack of maintenance on the cooler groups, which caused water starvation and overheating. Cooling equipment accounted for just over one third of all failures on the Swindon locomotives, electrical and control equipment causing a similar proportion. Hydraulic transmissions, which were fairly reliable, accounted for just over 6% of failures, and train-heating boilers 5%. A major B-B 'Warship' problem was rough riding at speeds above 80mph — a fault attributable to insufficient lateral bogie movement. A major redesign was required to rectify the problem, and during this time the maximum service speed was reduced by 10mph. The MAN engines were more problematical, with split exhaust manifolds being a perennial fault. Exhaust blowers upset the pressure-charging mechanism, which impacted the engine itself. The locking plates on the big-end bearings were defective, and bolt failures led to serious internal damage. Many of the general B-B failures related to minor auxiliary accessories that were not swiftly attended to, which resulted in more serious damage being caused to major parts. In many cases thermostatic devices were faulty, allowing components to overheat. In the above context a 'failure' was defined as a fault that caused a lateness of five minutes or more for passenger trains or 10 minutes or more on freights. Despite all these problems (and many more not mentioned) the availability situation gradually improved.

During the mid-1960s the availability of the Swindon-built locomotives was sometimes 20% higher than that of the NBL equivalents, but at other times there was little to choose between them. As an example, in 1965 there was a 16% availability difference between the two types, the Swindon locomotives averaging a respectable 95,000 miles per annum and the NBLs 80,000. This compared favourably with 'King'-class steam locomotives, which averaged 55,000 miles per annum, and the 'Castle' class, at 50,000. In 1965 the 'Westerns' were covering 65,000 miles, the new Brush Type 4s (Class 47) 69,000 miles and the older diesel-electric 'Peaks' (Classes 45 and 46) only 57,000 miles — hardly an advertisement for diesel-electric traction! To be fair, the diesel-electrics spent more of their time hauling freight, which produced a lower mileage figure.

In spite of these figures the BR Board decided that diesel-hydraulics were not the way forward, labelling them as 'non-standard' and introducing a policy of limited maintenance — the beginning of the end. Under the 1965 National Traction Plan BR had declared its intention radically to reduce the number (and thus variety) of classes of diesel locomotive in service, most of the victims being Pilot Scheme designs that were not perpetuated. As a result the five A1A-A1A 'Warships' were withdrawn *en masse* on 20 December 1967. South Wales scrap-metal merchants eventually cut them all up (although No D601 was to survive as little more than a bodyshell until 1980 — see page 112). From 1968 these heavy 2,000hp locomotives would be known retrospectively (having by that time already been withdrawn) as Class 41s, while the Maybach-engined 2,200hp Swindon-built machines became Class 42s and the MAN-engined NBL examples Class 43s. It should be mentioned that a single Swindon-built locomotive was fitted with a pair of Paxman diesel engines but, curiously, was included in the Class 42 category.

Between 1968 and 1972 the entire fleet of 71 B-B locomotives was withdrawn from service. The process was slow, with only three examples disappearing from the stock lists in 1968, four in 1969, none in 1970 (!), a disastrous 45 locomotives in 1971 and the balance of 19 in 1972. Whilst the entire 'Warship' fleet lasted between eight and 13 years, their lack of longevity was due to corporate policy

decisions rather than any lack of potential, which was never exploited to the full. As we have seen, the 'Warships' frequently recorded annual mileages that were superior to those of the large numbers of Type 4 diesel-electric locomotives that were introduced in the 1960s. The locomotives had plenty of faults (and some of these were major, requiring an element of redesign), but overall, and bearing in mind the learning-curve for maintenance staff and drivers in the early days, the diesel-hydraulics were as reliable as their diesel-electric counterparts. There is no doubt that the 'Warships' were underrated, and, had their life term been extended, they would surely have provided a better return for the capital investment made. Nevertheless, they were very significant in the BR diesel-hydraulic story and played an important part in the 'dieselisation' process following the original Modernisation Plan of 1955.

Although Classes 41s and 43 are extinct a pair of Class 42s survive in preservation, so at least future generations can see, with perhaps a little imagination, what they missed in the early days of 'dieselisation', when Type 4 locomotives hauled proper trains and made all the right noises! I hope that you enjoy *The Power of the Warships* as much as I have enjoyed compiling it. My thanks go to a number of individuals who are mentioned in the Acknowledgements on page 112.

John A. M. Vaughan
Goring-by-Sea, West Sussex
May 2005

Below:
The first Swindon-designed 'Warship', built in consultation with German engine and transmission suppliers, was an altogether different proposition from the somewhat cumbersome A1A-A1A design. Weighing some 39 tons less than the original NBL product, the B-B 'Warships' also had a superior power output, of 2,200hp. The BR loading gauge was 10in lower and 16in narrower than the German standard, and the power units and other components had to be shoehorned into the stressed-skin bodyshell. This view depicts the first of the slick-looking Swindon machines, No D800 *Sir Brian Robertson. BR(WR)*

Left:

The first A1A-A1A 'Warship' emerged from the NBL works in November 1957. The engines and transmissions fitted to the first and second locomotives were built in Germany, but thereafter the assembly of components took place in the UK. The first locomotive to emerge, NBL Works No 27660 (later D600), worked test trains in Scotland, and in this early and rare view, recorded on 27 November 1957, the shiny new machine is seen approaching Lugton with three coaches *en route* from Glasgow to Kilmarnock. *C. R. Dick*

Left:

This photograph shows the original 'Warship', No D600, on further trials in Scotland in December 1957. The locomotive was delivered to the WR in January 1958. At this time the body was green, as were the end roof panels, but otherwise the roof was silver-grey; the bogies were black, there would soon be a white band along the bodywork at solebar level, and the buffer casings and nameplates were red. Note the silver buffers and the two oil 'tail' lamps. *NBL*

Right:

The original 'Warships' were fitted with two V12 MAN L12V18/21A engines, each rated at 1,000hp at 1,445rpm, and Voith L306r transmission units. There were two fuel tanks, with capacities of 475 and 325 gallons. These locomotives were 65ft long — 5ft longer than the later lightweight versions. The four driving axles had an axle load of 20 tons, and the two idling axles 19 tons. What was to become No D600 was photographed in some appalling Scottish weather at NBL's Queen's Park works in 1957, before delivery to BR. *NBL*

Above:
Once delivered to the WR No D600 worked a number of test trains, initially between Swindon and Gloucester, and on 19 March 1958 it first worked to its eventual home of Plymouth with a 10-coach test train from Swindon. This scene depicts a later test train from Swindon, on 18 May 1958, hauled by No D601 *Ark Royal.* The substantial train, consisting of 13 coaches plus dynamometer car, is seen at Aller Junction, near Newton Abbot. Within a month the locomotive would be working the crack 'Cornish Riviera Express'. *Ian Allan Library*

Left:
This piece of modern-traction history shows No D601 *Ark Royal* just out of its box on Wednesday 23 April 1958. The immaculate locomotive is seen passing the south signalbox at Oxford station with an evening Swindon–Oxford Carriage Sidings test train, comprising 10 coaches including the dynamometer car. Over the years the original 'Warships' averaged between 55,000 and 71,000 miles per annum, and engine changes were required every 7,000-8,000 hours — about once per year. *B. D. Winkett*

Above:
What would become known as the Class 42s were all built at the BR (ex-GWR) works at Swindon in Wiltshire, whereas the Class 43 locomotives were the product of NBL in Glasgow. The Class 42s had Maybach engines and Mekydro transmission sets, whereas the Class 43s had MAN engines and Voith transmissions. In this view of the erecting shop at Swindon two of the former are seen under construction in the foreground, with further locomotives visible in the distance, while steam locomotives continued to be overhauled, that nearest the camera being 'Castle' 4-6-0 No 5024 *Carew Castle*.
C. J. Marsden collection

Left:
The construction of the 'Warships' started with two tubes, 6½in in diameter and ³⁄₁₆in thick, that ran almost the entire length of the locomotive. There were cross-stretchers made of steel plate welded to longitudinals outside and between the tubes, with a deck plate, drag boxes and buffer-beams. The bodyside frame members were welded to this structure, most of which was stress-bearing. In this view recorded at Swindon Works up to 10 locomotives are under construction. Most would be in service for little more than a decade. *Author's collection*

Right:
Although this snap of what was to become No D800 is technically deficient, it is a fun picture and shows four technicians leaning from the windows, including (unusually) one of the two bodyside windows. The picture was taken at Swindon on 6 June 1958, with the locomotive yet to receive its final paintwork.
The production locomotives cost between £119,000 and £122,000 to build, but the first three examples cost as much as £143,000. The NBL equivalents each cost £115,000, but they were less successful than the Swindon product. *John Lamb*

Below:
On 14 July 1958 the first lightweight B-B diesel-hydraulic (as distinct from the 117-ton A1A-A1A 'D600s'), No D800, was named *Sir Brian Robertson* (after the Chairman of the BTC). The locomotive incorporated steam-age white headcode discs, and behind the headboard was a bracket for the attachment of train-identification numbers. The truly immaculate machine is seen at Swindon just after naming. It would be at work as early as 26 July, heading a special train from Paddington to Cardiff.
British Transport Commission

Above:
In the early days the 'Warships' used train-indicator letters and numbers from the steam age, the five A1A-A1A examples and the first 13 B-B machines (Nos D800-12) being fitted with cab-end brackets for the purpose. In this scene recorded on 30 June 1960 No D805 *Benbow* displays a London Midland Region (LMR) headcode as it passes Shaldon with a Penzance–Manchester train composed of maroon LMR coaching stock. *Michael Mensing*

Below:
Displaying express-passenger headcode discs and code 'N45' (relating to the northbound 'Devonian'), No D805 *Benbow* powers through Teignmouth on 23 June 1960. The B-B 'Warships' were all delivered in BR green livery with a white stripe between the cab doors, although Nos D859-65 emerged from works with a small yellow warning panel on each end. *Michael Mensing*

Left:
Once the first 12 Swindon-built B-B 'Warships' had been delivered the original A1A-A1A locomotives were often relegated to rosters within the counties of Devon and Cornwall, and their appearances on top-link Paddington to West Country express workings diminished. However, on 6 June 1960 No D601 *Ark Royal* was entrusted to a Midlands-bound train, seen here at Exeter St Davids. Two years earlier this locomotive would have been entrusted with the 'Cornish Riviera' or the 'Royal Duchy'. *C. P. Boocock*

Right:
No D803 *Albion* entered traffic on 16 March 1959, and from this locomotive right through to No D870 *Zulu* the names of the 'Warships' were in alphabetical order, with the sole exception of No D812, intended to be *Despatch* but instead named *The Royal Naval Reserve 1859-1959*. On 10 September 1959 *Albion* runs along the sea wall at Dawlish with a Paddington-bound express. *C. J. Marsden collection*

Left:
On a summer afternoon in 1959 No D811 *Daring* sweeps through the curves at Powderham with a down inter-regional train. The TOPS designations — Classes 41, 42 and 43 — were not part of the BR vocabulary until the autumn of 1968, and the 'Class 41' label was applied retrospectively, after withdrawal of the fleet. Following the end of steam traction on BR the 'D' prefix to diesel locomotives' numbers (and the 'E' on electric locomotives, for that matter) was dropped, *Daring* becoming simply 811. *J. Davenport*

Swindon Works

Above:
It was entirely appropriate in the eyes of the majority of enthusiasts that many of the distinctive diesel-hydraulic locomotives that had a very strong regional identity should be built at Swindon Works. The establishment had a first-rate reputation and had its origins in the very early days of the Great Western Railway. This magnificent study well illustrates the steam-to-diesel transition and dates back to 14 March 1962. From left to right are No 5000 *Launceston Castle*, No 4093 *Dunster Castle* and No D869 *Zest*. M. Edwards

Right:
The 'Warships' covered many hundreds of thousands of miles in service, and inevitably each locomotive visited works for major overhaul at regular intervals. During their lifetime some locomotives, such as No D603, accumulated barely 500,000 miles 'on the clock', while some of the Swindon-built B-Bs achieved over 1 million miles. During that time the locomotives would have visited Swindon Works several times. Here NBL 'Warship' No D864 *Zambesi* has had its bodywork rubbed down for priming, and some accident damage has been cut out for replating. *C. J. Marsden collection*

Above:
A total of 38 B-B 'Warships' were built at Swindon Works between 1958 and 1961. The original order, placed in January 1956, was for just three locomotives (Swindon lot No 428), but an order for a further 30 locomotives (lot No 437) was placed in February 1957, to be followed by a final order for five locomotives (Swindon lot No 448) in April 1959. In addition 33 locomotives were built by NBL at Glasgow between 1960 and 1962. However, by the mid-1960s Swindon Works was overhauling members of the entire class, including the NBL examples. In this view No D852 *Tenacious*, resplendent in its new paint job, poses for the camera at Swindon. *Ian Allan Library*

Left:
This photograph illustrates a 'one-off' in the ranks of the Swindon-built 'Warships', No D830 *Majestic*, which was fitted with a pair of Paxman engines. At 2,270hp the locomotive was marginally more powerful than its sister machines, despite weighing nearly a ton less (and three tons less than the NBL-built version). The locomotive travelled half the mileage of other machines because when it failed a shortage of spares resulted in its being sidelined for weeks at a time. The locomotive is being refuelled in Swindon Works yard. *C. J. Marsden collection*

Above:
At the end of the diesel-hydraulic era in the late 1970s these three locomotives could be seen around the turntable at Swindon Works. No D821 *Greyhound* had just been purchased privately, No 818 *Glory* was missing major components and had been used on exercises by apprentices, and Class 35 'Hymek' No D7029 was also destined for preservation. Sadly *Glory* was eventually cut up, with the result that there are just two Class 42 'Warships' (and no Class 41s or 43s) in preservation. *John Vaughan*

Steam and Diesel

Above:
Under the BTC Modernisation Plan and the BR (motive power) Pilot Scheme a total of 130 locomotives were required for the complete 'dieselisation' of lines west of Newton Abbot in Devon and the whole of Cornwall. The most difficult stretch of line was over the South Devon banks where, in the days of steam, most express trains were double-headed. It was clear, despite the superior tractive effort of the diesels, that during the transitional period steam would at times have to work in tandem with diesel locomotives. In June 1958 trials commenced with No D601 working in turn with 'Hall' 4-6-0 No 4905 *Barton Hall*, 'Castle' 4-6-0 No 7000 *Viscount Portal* and 'Manor' 4-6-0 No 7813 *Freshford Manor*. In this magnificent study recorded on 4 July 1959 'King' 4-6-0 No 6018 *King Henry VI* double-heads 'Warship' No D602 *Bulldog* away from Newton Abbot with the 10.35 Paddington–Penzance. *D. S. Fish*

Right:
On Saturday 28 July 1962, in the days when full-length trains ran on our railways, the unusual pairing of 'County' 4-6-0 No 1009 *County of Carmarthen* and Swindon-built 'Warship' No D823 *Hermes* power the 13-coach 10.5 Penzance–Manchester, the duo being photographed between Brent and Totnes. The sound of the sharp beat of the two-cylinder steam locomotive and the two high-revving V12 Maybach engines of the diesel must have been memorable!
D. Ian Wood

Left:
Sometimes the double-heading of steam and diesel locomotives had little to do with train loading and everything to do with diesel-locomotive failure! On 26 September 1959 it was, somewhat embarrassingly, the 'Cornish Riviera Limited' that was in trouble as it passed through the centre road at Exeter St Davids some 45 minutes late behind failed train engine No D601 *Ark Royal* and rescuing 'Modified Hall' steam locomotive No 6995 *Benthall Hall*. On the right 'Small Prairie' No 5524 pauses with a down local. *P. Q. Treloar*

Above:
Steam/diesel double-heading occurred regularly in Cornwall, especially on the heaviest trains and notably on holiday trains on the demanding Newquay branch. Climbing up the 1-in-74/61 gradient from Hayle towards Angarrack with the up 'Royal Duchy' on 14 April 1960 are 'Grange' 4-6-0 No 6824 *Ashley Grange* and 'Warship' No D815 *Druid*. It is interesting to recall that as *Druid* was on the production line Swindon Works so too was '9F' 2-10-0 No 92220 *Evening Star*, the last steam locomotive built for use on BR. *P. Q. Treloar*

Above:

The maximum permitted load over the South Devon banks for a Type 4 diesel locomotive was significantly superior to that for even the most powerful WR steam locomotive. For example, a 'Castle' could take a load of 315 tons unaided over the South Devon banks, a 'King 385 tons, an original 'Warship' over 400 tons and a 2,700hp Class 50 580 tons! Whatever the capabilities of the locomotives, 'Hall' No 5929 *Hanham Hall* is making an obvious contribution to the last few yards of the climb to Dainton Tunnel, with No D805 *Benbow* contributing 2,200hp (less at the rail). *Maurice Dart collection*

Below:

A really stirring sight — of a kind that could be witnessed for only a short period in the late 1950s — is this view of 'King' four-cylinder 4-6-0 No 6018 *King Henry VI* and 16-month-old A1A-A1A 'Warship' No D601 *Ark Royal* both vigorously attacking the 1-in-57/46/41/36 climb between Stoneycombe and Dainton, west of Newton Abbot, on 1 August 1959. The train is the 10.35 Paddington–Penzance. Within a few years such trains would be hugely accelerated as a direct result of 'dieselisation' and lighter train loadings. *G. England*

A group of passengers at Paddington seem transfixed by the sight of A1A-A1A 'Warship' No D600 *Active* at the head of the down 'Cornish Riviera Express' on 21 March 1959. The photograph has a misty 'steam age' atmosphere, thanks to the steam-era train headboard and the slight leak (under the leading coach) from the locomotive's train-heating boiler, which was obviously in good working order. *Michael Mensing*

This photograph of the 'Cornish Riviera Express' at Paddington has been published previously, but despite featuring diesel traction the scene looks remarkably dated and simply had to be included for posterity. No D600 was the first named diesel in BR ownership, and notwithstanding trials with prototype diesels in the 1950s its arrival on the WR heralded a new generation of motive power. Following trial runs the original, heavy (117-ton) 'Warships' started working such expresses regularly from July 1958. *Ian Allan Library*

Once the B-B 'Warships' came on stream front-line use of the A1A-A1A examples gradually diminished. The later locomotives were lighter and more powerful and certainly more reliable than the original 117-tonners. In October 1958 No D801 was timed at 103mph on test, so with a 90mph service speed there was always plenty of potential speed in hand. No D853 *Thruster*, seen at Paddington, would not achieve such speeds with the down 'Rivo' on 21 October 1961. *Michael Mensing*

Vintage Sea Wall Views

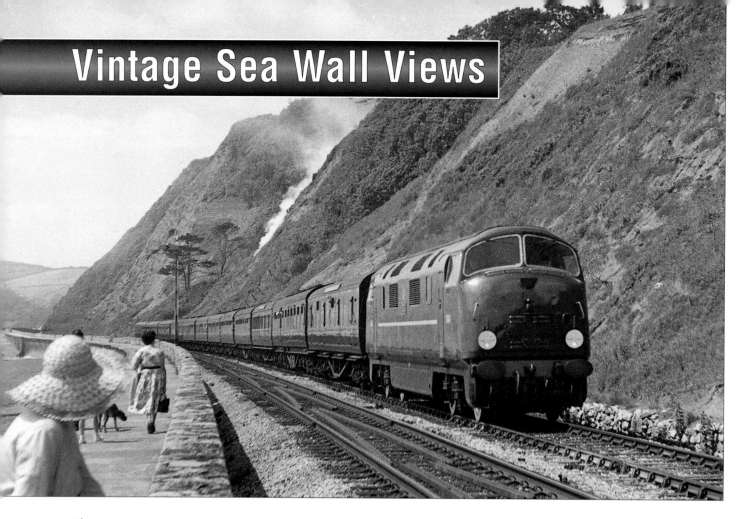

Above:

For many years railway photographers have flocked to the famous sea wall between Dawlish Warren and Teignmouth, in South Devon. The reason is obvious — the combination of great scenery and great views of trains from a very close (but safe) distance. Showing an express-passenger headcode but without identifying numerals is No D804 *Avenger* on 18 June 1959, then just two months old, with an inter-regional train for the North of England. *Michael Mensing*

Left:

This wonderful period scene near Teignmouth shows not only an admiring couple in 1950s summer attire and a splendid working wooden distant signal but also a slightly grubby 2,000hp NBL/MAN 'Warship', No D602 *Bulldog*, working what is believed to be the 6.25am Penzance–Paddington of 28 June 1960. In their first couple of years Nos D600 and D601, which had German-assembled engines, travelled about 150,000 miles, but as they were demoted from Class 1 trains this mileage more than halved. The mileage covered by Nos D602-4 was lower, as the UK-assembled components were allegedly not as reliable. *Michael Mensing*

Right:
The number of this Swindon-built locomotive was not recorded, but its train-headcode roller blinds reveal that it was not from the D800-12 series; from No D813 all 'Warships' were fitted with four-character roller blinds, and eventually the earlier locomotives were similarly modified. Five coaches and two mail vans head west at Teignmouth on the morning of 19 June 1960. *Michael Mensing*

Below:
Another 'proper' train of 13 coaches, providing between 700 and 750 seats, skirts the River Teign in the summer of 1960 behind Swindon-built No D814 *Dragon.* Some of the 'Warships' had Spanner train-heating boilers, others Stone-Vapor, but none was ever fitted with electric train heating, which would have been required had these locomotives lasted much beyond 1972. *J. Davenport*

Left:
When the various types of 'Warship' were delivered purpose-built maintenance facilities for diesel locomotives had not been built, and they were obliged to share existing steam sheds. Although the risks should not be exaggerated, electrical components were vulnerable in such dirty surroundings. At some locations parts of a steam shed were dedicated to the exclusive use of diesels, but this was not always the case. Eventually new depots at Plymouth Laira and Cardiff Canton were designated as heavy-maintenance centres, while Newton Abbot, Landore (Swansea) and Old Oak Common (in London) were to be planned-maintenance facilities. Here four 'Warships', including No D847 *Strongbow* on the left, share almost clinical conditions at Newton Abbot on 10 May 1962.
C. J. Marsden collection

Newton Abbot Diesel Depot

Above:
A remarkable early line-up of diesel-hydraulic types at
Newton Abbot in April 1963, a single 'Warship' being
surrounded by NBL 'D63xx' (Class 22) and Beyer-Peacock
'Hymek' (Class 35) locomotives, all in green livery. For some
time the old steam facilities and the new diesel installation
existed side by side, witness the water column to the left of
the 'Warship' and the old bullhead rail in the foreground.
Newton Abbot retained some of its steam-age buildings,
which were refurbished for diesel use. A new washing plant
was installed as late as 1963. *Maurice Dart collection*

Below:
This photograph, with No D844 *Spartan* on the right,
is included to illustrate the spotless conditions at the new
Newton Abbot diesel depot. In addition to the original list,
servicing was later undertaken at both Bristol Bath Road
and Ebbw Junction, but for major overhauls the 'Warships'
returned to Swindon Works. By the 1970s Newton Abbot
depot had lost its locomotive allocation, and it would
eventually close completely, all Devon activity being
centralised at Plymouth Laira.
C. J. Marsden collection

Left:
The purpose-built diesel depot at
Plymouth Laira opened partially in
1960 and fully in 1961, whereupon
the old steam shed was demolished.
In the days of steam the shed at
Newton Abbot had been a busy one,
but the authorities failed to appreciate
fully that, with main-line diesels
running through from Paddington to
Plymouth or Penzance and back in
one diagram, the new depot would be
permanently in the shadow of Laira,
and within a year or two of its opening
Newton Abbot was effectively
demoted in importance. No D829
Magpie stands at Newton Abbot's
refuelling facility as the driver says
"Fill her up, mate!". *C. J. Marsden
collection*

Headboards

Left:
A pleasant leftover from the days of steam was the use of headboards on the majority of named trains on the WR. The most famous was the 'Cornish Riviera Express', but there were many others, such as the 'Torbay Express', the 'Mayflower', the 'Royal Duchy', the 'Golden Hind' and the 'Bristolian'. Having just arrived at Kingswear, the driver of No D817 *Foxhound* removes the train's cast metal headboard on 28 July 1960. *M. D. Cresswell*

Left:
The winter of 1962/3 was one of the most severe on record, and the WR had to operate in adverse conditions. The speed of No D805 *Benbow* with the up 'Mayflower' is sufficient to blow some of the snow covering from the up to the down road on the approach to Taplow in February 1962. Judging from the equipment box there has been a snowfall of at least six inches. The headboard has a galleon above the train title.
C. J. Marsden collection

Right:
With a rake of both chocolate-and-cream and maroon coaches, No D811 *Daring* heads for Fairwood Junction, just west of Westbury, with the down 'Torbay Express' on 28 April 1962. The locomotive was the penultimate machine to be fitted with the old-style bracket, to which is attached the train's 'C39' code. The locomotive's headboard is supplemented by carriage boards at roof level. Westbury station can just be glimpsed above the leading cab. *G. A. Richardson*

Above:
Sporting the later (and final) style of headboard, No 801 *Vanguard* looks to be in good form as it sweeps into Gwinear Road station on 15 May 1959 with the down 'Cornish Riviera Express'. Passengers would change trains here for the branch train down to Helston, but the branch line closed in November 1962 followed by the main-line station in October 1964. Note the sailor (on the up platform), who is no doubt returning to Plymouth after a home visit.
Michael Mensing

Left:
A photograph recalling those wonderful summer days of times past, when pleasures were simple and children still waved at passing trains. In the summer of 1959 four youngsters, who were presumably out for a stroll near Respryn Bridge, west of Bodmin Road station, wave to the driver of a down 'Warship', who can be seen reciprocating with enthusiasm. Embellishments include the 'Cornish Riviera Express' headboard, the train-indicator number (416) and a pair of headcode discs. *Author's collection*

Left:
Photographed in April 1960 just a few yards from the end of its long journey from Paddington, the down 'Cornish Riviera Express' enters Penzance behind A1A-A1A 'Warship' No D604 *Cossack*. The headboard seems to have become dislodged, but in fact the attachment bracket on the 'D600s' was off-centre. As the years went by it became increasingly difficult to get spares for these locomotives, but what was truly scandalous was the fact that all save No D603 received a full overhaul at Swindon Works during 1967, their last year of service. *P. Q. Treloar*

Left:
In June 1959 the 'Bristolian' schedule was significantly improved, such was the success of the 'Warships' performance, the 117.6 miles from Paddington to Bristol being reeled off in just 100 minutes. Indeed, such was the WR's confidence in the type that No D804 was noted on the train on its first day of service. Here, on 22 September 1961, NBL-built No D839 *Relentless* heads the up 12-coach 'Bristolian' past Moreton, just east of Didcot. In the background grubby 'WD' 2-8-0 No 90565 has just left the extensive goods yard, long since abandoned. *Michael Mensing*

Left:
There had been a steam shed at Old Oak Common for many years. The depot was famous for its magnificent covered turntables, which simply oozed atmosphere until steam traction was withdrawn in 1964/5. Despite the 'dieselisation' of the WR from 1958 it is surprising to relate that the building of a diesel facility did not start until 1964. The original 'Warships' were allocated to Plymouth Laira for the whole of their working lives except for a very short stay in South Wales in 1967, but eventually the sight of A1A-A1A machines such as No D604 *Cossack* at Old Oak Common would become a rarity. *B. Roberts*

Old Oak Common

Left:
In August 1991 OOC held a public open day, and a large number of diesel exhibits were imported, including this wonderful trio of diesel-hydraulics from the 'modern' traction past. Recalling the early 1960s are, from left to right, Class 35 'Hymek' No D7018, Class 42 'Warship' No D821 *Greyhound*, Class 52 'Western' No D1015 *Western Champion* and, bringing the scene back to modern reality, GM Class 59 No 59001 *Yeoman Endeavour*. *P. G. Barnes*

Right:
Although the diesel-servicing shed at OOC was in operation in January 1965 the depot was not completed and formally opened until 20 October. In this fine portrait No D800 *Sir Brian Robertson* shares steam-age accommodation with half a dozen English Electric (Class 08) shunters. The first three Swindon-built 'Warships' differed in many ways from the rest of the fleet, having, for example, non-standard torque-converters and six- (rather than seven-) notch controllers; further, they could not work in multiple with others in the class. Nos D800-2 were thus the first B-B examples to be withdrawn, all three succumbing in 1968. *C. R. L. Coles*

Above:
By the beginning of 1962 BR had decided that its diesel locomotives should be more visible, especially to permanent-way workers, and the last seven NBL 'Warships', Nos D859-65, were delivered in BR standard green but with a small yellow warning panel around the headcode panels. Similar panels were later applied to other members of the class, such as No D827 *Kelly*, seen here climbing up to Rattery Tunnel in Devon on 28 July 1962 with the 11.20 Newquay–Birmingham. Note the two splendid LNER/Eastern Region teak coaches behind the locomotive. *D. Ian Wood*

Left:
A well-executed photograph at a familiar location is this shot of NBL/MAN-engined No D848 *Sultan*, sporting a small yellow warning panel, as it heads the up 'Devonian' through Teignmouth on 12 June 1967. Although Swindon- and NBL-built versions both featured two 12-cylinder high-speed engines the Maybach and MAN power units were not interchangeable. Note the WR lower-quadrant signals on the down road. *G. F. Gillham*

Above:

A very unusual picture showing No D823 *Hermes* in maroon livery with a small warning panel. Working engineers' train 9Z67 on 12 June 1967, the locomotive is propelling the wagons along the up road of the WR main line near Teignmouth. Four track workers are riding 'outboard' in one of the wagons, and a chap in a flat hat and sports jacket has emerged from the driver's door! Heavy seas regularly breach the wall, a major washout occurring in October 2004.
G. F. Gillham

Right:

The line from Aller Junction to Torquay, Paignton and Kingswear was a regular stamping-ground for the 'Warships'. Passing Gasworks Sidings on 4 September 1965 with the 13-coach 07.50 Paddington–Paignton express is No D859 *Vanquisher*. The locomotive is in green livery with small warning panels. Note the two sidings on the left, containing four-wheeled coal wagons, in an era that considerably preceded North Sea gas. *A. N. Yeates*

Above:

The loop on the Plymouth line at Aller Junction has long since been removed, but on 14 July 1969 freight trains were regularly switched into the loop to allow passenger trains to pass. Another local feature that has now gone was Stoneycombe Quarry, a mile or two to the west, where stone and ballast were once loaded into hopper wagons for transportation by rail. Heading for Stoneycombe is No D845 *Sprightly* with vacuum-braked wagons and a 'Shark' brake van. *G. F. Gillham*

Left:
The original, heavy A1A-A1A 'Warships' also had small yellow warning panels applied in the early 1960s. No D601 is seen on pilot duties at Plymouth North Road on 3 September 1964. Headcode discs were retained at this time, train-indicator panels not being fitted until later in the decade. Only No D600 would (eventually) gain full yellow ends, and only Nos D600 and D602 received blue livery. *G. F. Gillham*

Right:
Class 42 'Warships' were used in multiple from 1968, when the fastest express schedules were greatly accelerated. Two Class 42s were also requested by the Stephenson Locomotive Society, for its 'Dart Valley Special' of 17 May 1969; sporting chartex headcode 1Z17, No D804 *Avenger* waits to leave Paddington with sister locomotive No D868 *Zephyr* at the head of the 08.17 for Totnes. *R. F. Roberts / SLS collection*

Above:
The terminus of Paddington has a great tradition going back to the mid-19th century — the days of Brunel and the broad gauge. Even in the diesel era many WR headquarters offices were located at Paddington, including that of the Locomotive Development Engineer. Seen arriving at the London terminus on 31 January 1959 with the 6.25am from Penzance is No D801 *Vanguard*. The locomotive was then just two months old, having been introduced to traffic in November 1958, some three months after No D800. *Michael Mensing*

Above:
After leaving Paddington trains passed Royal Oak and a stabling and refuelling point at Ranelagh Road. Passing London Transport Hammersmith lines on the right and some early container wagons at the distribution depot on the left No D850 *Swift* powers a Torquay train out of the Metropolis on 21 April 1971. BR blue livery became standard from 1967, while full yellow ends were applied not only to blue locomotives but also to a handful of green and maroon examples. *P. H. Groom*

Left:
The new 1968 West Country timetable saw a significant reduction in journey times for selected trains, which featured double-headed Class 42s working in multiple. For the first time some trains were booked to cover the 225½ miles from Paddington to Plymouth in 225 minutes — an average speed in excess of 60mph. Originally Nos D822-9/31/2/66-8 were allocated for such duties, although non-availability resulted in a corruption of the designated 'Warship' roster. Getting to grips with the 12-coach 14.30 Paddington–Penzance at West Ealing on 29 May 1968 are No D868 *Zephyr* and an unidentified sister locomotive. *John Cooper-Smith*

Above:
No fewer than 13 maroon coaches present a tough prospect for green No D823 *Hermes*, seen passing Iver, Bucks, with a train from the West Country on 11 April 1964. The 'Warships' were passed to travel at 90mph, but due to chronic bogie vibration at speeds above 80mph they were speed-restricted for some time while bogie modifications were undertaken. The original bogie design had allowed insufficient lateral motion, which caused severe oscillation. *G. J. Jefferson*

Below:
A 'Warship' diesel locomotive double-heading a steam locomotive with the diesel leading was less common than the reverse order. However, on Saturday 11 March 1961 No D825 *Intrepid* piloted 'Castle' No 5011 *Tintagel Castle* as far as Swindon with the 2.55pm Paddington–Swansea express, seen passing through Hayes & Harlington station. *M. Pope*

Left:
Not only were the NBL B-B 'Warships' less reliable than the Swindon examples, but also their exhaust manifolds had a propensity to crack, which resulted in fumes in the cab, thereby creating a potential danger for drivers. Approaching West Drayton on 4 February 1964 is No D856 *Trojan* with the 9.45am Paddington–Weston-super-Mare express. *G. J. Jefferson*

Left:
Although 'Warships' were not generally used on freight trains until the spring of 1960 they were equally at home on freight workings as they were on express passenger trains. The B-B locomotives did not have the brake force of the heavier A1A-A1A type, but most freight trains were becoming fitted with a continuous brake, so any problems diminished. Heading a delightful load of four-wheelers at Hayes & Harlington on 19 October 1963 is 2,200hp No D820 *Grenville*. The Class 5 working is bound for Exeter Riverside. *Brian Stephenson*

Left:
The Maybach diesel engine was remarkably reliable, but poorly maintained cooler groups were the cause of a large number of cracked cylinder heads, resulting in engine overheating. Of all the casualties experienced with Swindon-built 'Warships', one third related to cooling equipment, and another third to electrical controls and apparatus; braking equipment caused another 10% of the problems, while engines and transmissions together accounted for less than 9% of train failures. Here an absolutely brand-new Maybach-engined machine speeds past Southall depot with a down Class 3 parcels train. *Ian Allan Library*

Right:
Its steam-age headcode discs denoting a down parcels train, a resplendent No D805 *Benbow* approaches Waltham St Lawrence, near Twyford, on 14 May 1959. The locomotive had entered traffic only the previous day — no doubt the photographer considered that he had secured a real 'scoop'! *D. A. Regan*

Above:
A wonderful view of railway infrastructure near Reading in the late 1950s as No D812 *The Royal Naval Reserve 1859-1959* passes with a down express. This was the only locomotive between Nos D803 and D870 that was not named in strict alphabetical order. Note not only the lower-quadrant semaphore signals but also the large number of point rods (on the left) and the plethora of signal wires (right). *Ian Allan Library*

Above:
An all-time favourite photographic location on the WR main line has been Sonning Cutting, just east of Reading, where trains in action have been recorded on film for well over a century. On 5 July 1968 No D832 *Onslaught* toys with just seven coaches forming an up express as a Brush Type 4 toils with a freight on the up slow line. *John Cooper-Smith*

Left:
On the same date as the previous photograph but seen one bridge to the east is NBL 'Warship' No D854 *Tiger* negotiating Sonning Cutting with a coal train for West Drayton. The train is almost certainly vacuum-fitted, but a brake van brings up the rear of the formation nevertheless. The two Sonning pictures admirably demonstrate the versatility of the 'Warships'. *John Cooper-Smith*

Above:
No D802 *Formidable* cost £143,000 to build, and the WR wasted no time in getting some of its money back by diagramming the new locomotive on the 'Cornish Riviera Express', the down working being seen here in September 1960. Unusually this prestigious train has an interesting compartment coach marshalled between the locomotive and the Mk 1 stock. Although the distant signal is 'off' the train will soon be slowing for Reading before heading down the Berks & Hants line. *Ian Allan Library*

Right:
This special Class 4 fitted freight looks suspiciously like a load of Mk II Ford Cortinas, Zephyrs and Zodiacs, seen heading west through Sonning Cutting on the down slow road on 28 May 1969 behind No D867 *Zenith*. The locomotive is seen in maroon livery, which was first applied to a 'Warship' in 1965. Three locomotives were withdrawn in this livery — Nos D801 *Vanguard*, D840 *Resistance* and D848 *Sultan*. *John Cooper-Smith*

Above:

An up express due to leave Newbury at 11.55 arrives from the West Country behind a pair of Swindon-built 'Warships', Nos D824 *Highflyer* and D825 *Intrepid*, on 9 March 1968. A white diamond, denoting the multiple-working coupling code, can be seen on the buffer-beam of the lead locomotive. The multiple-working controls utilised 36-wire jumper cables. This was the heyday of Mk 1 coaches, and Mark 2b coaches were about to be introduced. Vacuum versus air brakes and steam versus electrical train heating would soon become an issue, as compatible locomotives would be required for the new stock.
D. Bullock

Below:

Contrasting with a steam locomotive, which needed to be coaled and watered at frequent intervals, a 'Warship' could work from Paddington to Penzance and back without refuelling. The 'D800s' had a fuel consumption of 1mpg, giving a 700-mile range, although diesel sludge could accumulate at the bottom of fuel tanks, so the full capacity of 800 gallons was never exploited. The up 'Torbay Express' is passing the Kennet & Avon Canal just west of Hungerford behind No D808 *Centaur*.
J. C. Beckett

Right:
As long ago as 1964 there was continuously welded rail on concrete sleepers at Reading West. Travelling over the excellent permanent way near Southcote Junction on 12 September is No D854 *Tiger* with the down 'Cornish Riviera Express'. The locomotive entered traffic on 26 September 1961 and was withdrawn on 3 October 1971 — a life of exactly a decade. *G. M. Cashmore*

Left:
'Warships' hauled milk trains all over the WR, including, by way of example, workings in Devon from Totnes, in Cornwall from St Erth, Dalcoath and Lostwithiel, in Somerset from Chard Junction and over all routes from the West Country to Acton, Kensington and West Ealing in London. A down train of empty six-wheeled milk tankers is seen passing Hungerford Common on 29 May 1965 behind No D860 *Victorious. Michael Mensing*

Right:
During the last days of the 'Warships' some locomotives were withdrawn from service only to be reinstated when regional motive-power availability fell to a level where service commitments could not be fulfilled. No 829 *Magpie* was withdrawn, dumped on the 'store' line and had its nameplates ripped off only to be reinstated for a couple of months. Minus nameplates, the veteran was good enough to be entrusted on 22 July 1972 with the 14.30 Paddington–Paignton, seen at Wolfhall Junction, west of Bedwyn. The former alignment of the Midland & South Western Junction Railway is visible on the embankment above the last coach. *G. F. Bannister*

Above:
In the early 1960s the level of car ownership was a fraction of what it is today, and especially in the holiday season many trains to the West Country loaded to 13 coaches. Here train 1A62, the up 'Torbay Express', leaves the main line at Fairwood Junction and takes the loop line into Westbury station. The locomotive is the unique No D830 *Majestic*, fitted with a pair of Paxman (of Colchester) engines. Introduced in January 1961, it was an early candidate for withdrawal, which came in March 1969. *G. A. Richardson*

Left:
Although the majority of 'Warships' passing through Westbury over the years were on the West of England main line, they occasionally worked Class 2 (local) passenger trains between Bristol Temple Meads and Weymouth. By the time this photograph was taken, in January 1972, all of the Class 43s had been withdrawn, so this unidentified 'Warship' is a Maybach-engined Class 42. It is seen at the head of train 2V55, which has just arrived from the SR seaside terminus. *John Vaughan*

Right:
By 1964 many of the 'Warships' had accumulated enough miles on the clock to be in need of a full works overhaul. For this purpose the Maybach-engined examples travelled back to their birthplace at Swindon. Bringing a dull day to life, an absolutely ex-works No D826 *Jupiter* leaves Westbury station with a Plymouth–Paddington express on 8 June 1964. The locomotive has been outshopped in green with small yellow warning panel. The signalbox and the semaphores were removed *c*1980. *Derek Cross*

Above:
Defective train-heating boilers accounted for 10% of all 'Warship' failures. On 6 November 1960, its Stone-Vapor boiler having expired, No D824 *Highflyer* had to pull into Westbury with the down 'Cornish Riviera Express' for a steam locomotive to be attached as pilot. The roller-blind headcode panels are in use and showing the correct identification, the 'CRE' headboard having been abandoned. *A. Hobbs*

Left:
This photograph prominently features rocks and stone rather than a 'Warship' but is nevertheless historically interesting. Despite their low weight the B-B locomotives were used regularly on stone trains, and this official photograph produced by Foster Yeoman Ltd shows a rather tired-looking No D826 *Jupiter* at Merehead Quarry on 19 August 1970. On the right of the picture are empty wagons in position for loading, while just visible in the background is Torr Works. *Foster Yeoman*

Above:
A few miles west of Fairwood Junction, Westbury, is Clink Road Junction, on the outskirts of Frome. The main line bypasses the town station, but for stopping trains a loop is provided, visible here beyond the third coach, these lines also leading to Whatley Quarry and the old Radstock branch. With the driver of No D849 *Superb* exchanging waves with the permanent-way gang, Class 1 express 1A42 makes for London on 10 August 1962. *G. A. Richardson*

Right:
The road is clear for 2,000hp NBL/MAN 'Warship' No D604 *Cossack*, proudly heading the down 'Cornish Riviera Express' on the approach to Cogload Junction, north of Taunton, on 6 June 1960. By this time these heavy locomotives, which had inferior performance but gave a better ride than their 2,200hp lightweight namesakes, were being relegated from the most prestigious trains to more menial duties in west Devon and Cornwall. *G. J. Jefferson*

Below
No D811 *Daring*, the last 'Warship' to be fitted with a train-indicator bracket rather than roller blinds, is seen in original condition climbing Brewham Bank, to the west of Bruton, with the up 'Mayflower' on 27 July 1960. The photograph was taken from the old Somerset & Dorset Joint Railway line, which crossed the ex-GWR main line at this point. Note the incongruous Gresley LNER/ER coach immediately behind the locomotive. *G. A. Richardson*

Left:
In the early 1960s Taunton was a tremendous railway centre and an important railway crossroads. To the north, at Cogload Junction, the lines to London and Bristol (and the north) merged, while to the west, at Norton Fitzwarren, lines radiated to Exeter, Barnstaple and Minehead. Passing beneath a truly magnificent signal gantry on 6 August 1961 is 'Warship' No D823 *Hermes* with train 1N68 from Truro in Cornwall to Bradford in Yorkshire. The WR locomotive would work as far as Bristol. *D. P. Leckonby*

Left:
Another inter-regional working but this time speeding through Tiverton Junction, which was once the junction for Tiverton Town and Hemyock, the terminus of the Culm Valley branch line. No D816 *Eclipse* passes the now closed station on 12 September 1970 with a down express. The BR double-arrow on this all-blue locomotive is placed amidships below the nameplate, but some repaints had arrows on each cabside. *John Vaughan*

Left:
Just before the tunnel at Whiteball the main line passes from Somerset into Devon. On the Devon side of the summit No D861 *Vigilant* toils up the climb to Whiteball and passes the down freight loop with the 1E54 from Plymouth to Sheffield on 19 March 1970. Pictured in maroon livery with small yellow panel, the locomotive would be withdrawn with the last large batch of NBL machines in October 1971. *Ron Elsdon*

Right:
Taunton at 09.05 on a dull 3 January 1970 finds the station lights still on, giving the impression of a scene at dusk rather than dawn. The photograph is also unusual in showing that the output from the unidentified Class 42's boiler is being mostly wasted, as train-heating steam leaks appear to exist all the way along the rake of ageing Mk 1 stock. Again, the white diamond on the buffer-beam shows that the locomotive still has operational multiple-working equipment. *John Vaughan*

Above:
With a full yellow end and BR corporate blue livery a dirty No 808 *Centaur* arrives at Taunton on 22 August 1970 with what the photographer describes as the 08.10 Kensington Olympia–St Austell motorail train; it would seem that the driver has not taken the trouble to change the headcode from a previous working. The train is taking the down island platform road and judging by the 'on' distant signal will come to a halt at the platform. *H. W. Cater*

Left:
This photograph of Cowley Bridge Junction, north of Exeter, on 3 May 1964 is full of interest, featuring not only a three-vehicle Class 3 van train but also a 'Warship' sporting a small yellow warning panel *before* having its headcode brackets replaced by roller blinds. Note the correct headcode-disc display and the driver's tea can on the 'dashboard'. The former SR lines to Barnstaple and Okehampton can be seen above the locomotive. *M. J. Fox*

Left:
Motive power displaying a mix of liveries leaves Exeter St Davids with a Plymouth–Paddington express in 1968. A total of 4,400hp is unleashed as No D825 *Intrepid* in green and D822 *Hercules* in blue, working together in multiple, try to keep to the accelerated schedules introduced in the summer of that year. From 1968 drivers from Old Oak Common did not work west of Exeter, while those from Plymouth Laira did not work east of Taunton, resulting in crew changes on through trains at either Exeter or Taunton. *Ian Allan Library*

Left:
A view of the north end of Exeter St Davids station, recorded on 8 July 1970. At this time 'Warships' were a common sight at Exeter, not only on the WR main line but also on the SR Exeter–Waterloo services, which they took over in 1964 and worked until finally displaced in 1971.
R. F. Roberts / SLS collection

Right:
It was inevitable that with 'Warships' working London–Bristol/Weston-super-Mare services as well as London–Plymouth/Penzance trains they would be employed on inter-regional services and other trains between Taunton, Bristol and Birmingham. In March 1960 one of the first 13 Swindon-built 'Warships' speeds through Highbridge with the 10.23 Manchester–Plymouth. Crossing the main line behind the signalbox was the track from the Somerset & Dorset Joint Railway Highbridge station to the terminus at Burnham-on-Sea. *B. Perryman*

Taunton–Birmingham

Below:
Trains serving Weston-super-Mare must leave the main line and negotiate a long loop line from Worle Junction to Uphill Junction in order to call at the station. Southbound trains terminating at Weston simply leave the main line at Worle Junction to reach their seaside destination. The once double-track loop is now single-track outside the immediate vicinity of Weston station. Approaching Weston with the up 'Devonian' on 27 June 1962 is No D837 *Ramillies*. It would seem that a large bird has flown into one of the indicator panels, breaking the Perspex cover. *Michael Mensing*

Above:
A 1963 scene at Yatton station illustrates the transition from steam to diesel traction and the end of a significant era. On the down main line No D802 *Formidable* pauses with the 9.45am Paddington–Weston-super-Mare while '2MT' 2-6-2T No 41248 waits to depart with the 2.0pm to Witham via Wells. The GWR raised-letter running-in board proclaims 'YATTON — junction for CHEDDAR LINE AND CLEVEDON', these destinations being served by branch lines which would close in 1963 and 1966 respectively. *Leslie Sandler*

Left:
A sparkling shot of maroon 'Warship' No D858 *Valorous* passing a diminutive signalbox near Bedminster (to the south of Bristol) with train 1N37 — the northbound 'Devonian' — on 12 September 1968. By this time the five 'D600' 'Warships' had been withdrawn, a fate that was about to be shared by the first three 'D800s', and, however far away, the writing was clearly on the wall for the remainder. *John Cooper-Smith*

Above:
Passing lineside allotments at Weston-super-Mare on 4 July 1962 is Maybach-powered No D831 *Monarch* with a southbound train. Within 18 months the WR's diesel-hydraulic fleet would reach its peak, at 309 locomotives. *Michael Mensing*

Right:
Although in later years many inter-regional trains south of Bristol would produce the heavy 1Co-Co1 'Peak' diesel-electric locomotives of Classes 45 and 46, in September 1966, when this photograph was taken, WR diesel-hydraulics still ruled. Approaching Uphill Cutting, near Weston, is an unidentified 'Warship' with an express from Plymouth. *D. H. Cape*

Left:
North of Bristol Temple Meads is Stoke Gifford, which was to become the site of Bristol Parkway station. On 19 August 1967 NBL-built No D849 *Superb* runs along the down road light-engine, with oil tail-lamp *in situ*. Beyond the signalbox the lines to the Severn Tunnel and South Wales separate from the route down to Bristol Temple Meads and the West Country. *G. R. Hounsell*

Centre left:
As previously mentioned, purpose-built diesel depots were not ready in time for the delivery of the first main-line diesels, but by 9 August 1961 the first portion of Bristol Bath Road depot had been completed, as seen here. Two 'Warships', including No D837 *Ramillies* (on the right), share the accommodation with a 'Peak'. *B. A. Haresnape*

Below:
There is plenty of human interest in this scene at the down end of Bristol Temple Meads station. Arriving with an inter-regional train for the Midlands is No D813 *Diadem*, in standard BR blue livery with full yellow ends and BR logos on each cab. The sign that looks like a gradient post below the leading cab reads simply 'GANG 31' and 'GANG 31A'. *P. J. Fowler*

Right:

A superbly framed photograph taken from the tranquillity of Victoria Park, Bristol, near Temple Meads station, shows NBL No D863 *Warrior* leaving the city with a clear road ahead on the 08.20 Bristol–Plymouth of 17 August 1968. No passengers are visible in the leading maroon Mk 1 BSK coach. *P. J. Fowler*

Right:

When delivered all of the B-B 'Warships' had the BR lion-and-wheel totem crest placed amidships immediately above their nameplates. The cab ends of the B-B 'Warships' displayed a family likeness to the German 'V200' diesel-hydraulic locomotives, but because the British loading gauge was restricted and because certain equipment was located in the nose there were key differences. No D817 *Foxhound* is seen at Bristol Temple Meads. *Ian Allan Library*

Right:

There has been an enormous amount of track and signalling rationalisation at Narroways Hill Junction, north of Bristol, since this photograph was taken on 8 May 1969. The main line in the foreground is now merely double-track, the Severn Beach branch on the right is now single-track, and the sidings in the background have long since been lifted. No D803 *Albion* tackles the climb from Stapleton Road with the 12.35 Malago Vale–Old Oak Common vans. The leading utility van has a 60mph maximum speed, which will dictate the speed of the train. *D. H. Ballantyne*

Left:
Regrettably the old MR Gloucester Eastgate station is no longer with us, all traffic now being centred on the ex-GWR Central station — an operating inconvenience, because north–south trains calling at Gloucester have to reverse. Seen pausing at Eastgate is No 854 *Tiger* with the 11.20 Paignton–Manchester relief on 30 July 1971, by which time the locomotive had but two months to 'live'.
David Wharton

Right:
This record shot taken at Gloucester's Horton Road depot shows No 845 *Sprightly* in its final BR livery on 18 March 1970. Blue livery was ultimately applied to 63 'Warships', many being repainted from green to blue without ever appearing in maroon. *N. E. Preedy*

Right:
After delivery from the NBL works at Glasgow to the WR at Swindon in January 1958 the very first 'Warship', No D600 *Active*, was 'active' with Swindon–Gloucester test trains. The return journey, which included the climb to Sapperton Tunnel, was a good test for new machinery. In this picture taken on 28 March 1958 the locomotive is seen at Gloucester Central with its side access doors open. *P. J. Sharpe*

Right:
In the early days 'Warship' locomotives approached the Birmingham area mainly on the Birmingham Direct and Reading/Oxford lines from Paddington rather than via the inter-regional north–south route (see page 85). A leftover from the pre-nationalisation days of the Great Western Railway were the Paddington–Birkenhead workings, such as the 2.10pm from Paddington to Birkenhead, seen approaching Wellington (Salop) on 27 August 1962 behind No D817 *Foxhound. Michael Mensing*

Right:
Lurking in the cavernous gloom of the old ex-GWR Birmingham Snow Hill station on 13 October 1962 is No D827 *Kelly* with the 7.30am Shrewsbury–Paddington. The station eventually closed following the electrification of the LMR main line from Euston to Birmingham New Street, only for the track alignment to be reused many years later as part of a revised Birmingham suburban system. *Michael Mensing*

Right:
Although 'Warships' worked the Paddington–Birmingham services their reign was curtailed as Brush Type 4s and 'Westerns' began to arrive in large numbers. As early as August 1962 the 'Westerns' were working Paddington–Birmingham trains, and in November 1963 Brush Type 4s Nos D1682-8 were working Paddington–Wolverhampton trains, replacing the 'Westerns'! Strangely, 'Warships' were to have a final fling on Birmingham services towards the end of 1967. No D824 *Highflyer* heads a down train at Birmingham Snow Hill with a splendid 'Siphon G' van marshalled immediately behind the locomotive. *Ian Allan Library*

Left:
From March 1962 'Warships' appeared on the North & West route between Newport and Crewe via Shrewsbury. The locomotives appeared mostly on inter-regional services, many of which were routed via Hereford. The appearance of the first of the NBL 'D800s', No D833 *Panther*, is a credit to the WR's depot staff as the locomotive passes Brecon Junction signalbox, Hereford, on 1 May 1962 with the 9.10am Liverpool–Plymouth. *Anthony A. Vickers*

North & West Route to Crewe

Above:
Some inter-regional trains called at Newport station, often resulting in a change of locomotive, but others worked direct from Maindee East Junction to Maindee North Junction without calling at Newport, so that the locomotive that had taken the train from Bristol travelled through to Crewe. Bursting out of Dinmore Tunnel, north of Hereford, on 16 April 1963 is No D810 *Cockade* with the 9.05am Liverpool–Plymouth. *Anthony A. Vickers*

Above:
Framed by an oak tree near Ludlow in Shropshire, an unidentified NBL 'D800' heads towards Hereford with an inter-regional working from Liverpool on a dull day in August 1963. The North British Locomotive Co ceased trading *c*1967, but for some time previously certain spare parts were hard to come by, and once one of these locomotives failed it could be out of action for some time, unless another could be cannibalised. *J. R. Smith*

Right:
Although Worcester–Paddington services were worked by 'Warships' in 1964 and in 1969/70, at various other times they were in the hands of Class 35 'Hymeks' and, particularly, Class 47s. In later years, long after the 'Warships' had disappeared from the WR scene, Class 31s, 47s and 50s were diagrammed. At the delightful Hereford station No D846 *Steadfast* waits to depart with train 1A80, alias the 18.05 Hereford–Paddington, on 26 April 1969. *R. F. Roberts / SLS collection*

Left:
One of the most difficult photographs to secure is of an early 'Warship' with an original headcode frame featuring not only a small yellow warning panel but also with the steam-age numerals in place. On 15 May 1962 No D806 *Cambrian* obliged as it passed Red Hill Junction, south of Hereford, with the 9.10am Liverpool–Plymouth. *Anthony A. Vickers*

Left:
It would appear that the photographer was not the only enthusiast to record No D828 *Magnificent* passing Whitchurch (Salop) with the complex (and combined) Plymouth/Kingswear–Liverpool Lime Street/Glasgow Central on another Easter Monday, this time 15 April 1963. Note the impressive water tank, with water outlets for either platform. *Michael Mensing*

Left:
In days gone by Shrewsbury station had an overall roof with through and bay platforms and was a very busy railway hub, with trains radiating in half a dozen directions. Pictured on Easter Monday (23 April) 1962, No D831 *Monarch* has through coaches from both Liverpool and Manchester behind it as it awaits a 'right time' 11.20 departure for Plymouth. *R. D. Stephen*

Above:
The scenery in the Welsh Border country in the environs of Church Stretton rivals many parts of the UK, especially on a decent day. With the Long Mynd providing a backdrop, No D860 *Victorious* looks a little worse for wear as it powers a Liverpool–Plymouth train southwards on the old North & West route on 24 April 1964. *Derek Cross*

Right:
On 24 July 1962, shortly after the introduction of 'Warships' on the route, No D828 *Magnificent* enters 'foreign' territory at Crewe, having hauled the 8.0am Plymouth–Manchester throughout. At Crewe the locomotive would be detached to wait for a back-run to the West Country. The locomotive is seen under the wires, two small white plates below the windscreen warning train crews of the 25kV danger. *G. P. Brown*

Right:
Having arrived at Crewe from the south on 19 October 1963, No D838 *Rapid* has retired to Crewe North shed for a rest. To avoid their pre-heaters' draining the batteries 'Warship' locomotives were kept idling at depots and stabling points for lengthy periods of time. In the shed is an example of an English Electric Type 4 (Class 40), which typically had an annual mileage rate almost identical to that of an NBL 'D800' (but lower than that of a Swindon-built example). *Ian Allan Library*

Double-headers

Above:

It seems strange now, bearing in mind that diesel-hydraulics were deemed 'non-standard' by the BR Board, that as late as May 1968 the WR announced a dramatic revamp to its West of England timetable using pairs of Class 42 'Warships' in multiple, titling its press release 'BR's Most Powerful Trains for West Country'. The official photographer panned his camera to give the impression of high speed in this view featuring Nos D827 *Kelly* and D822 *Hercules*. An amusing choice of words stated that the 'top cruising speed [would be] 90mph'. *BR(WR)*

Below:

Pairs of 'Warships' set the tracks alight and broke many service-train records. Trains were scheduled to reach Exeter in 139 minutes at an *average* speed of 74.9mph; however, on occasions individual trains ran even faster, and on 5 May 1969 Nos D819 *Goliath* and D808 *Centaur* reached Exeter St Davids in 131min 30sec (at an average speed of 80mph) and Plymouth (225½ miles) in 203min (an average of 70mph) — seven minutes inside schedule. A Penzance–Paddington express is seen in Sonning Cutting on 15 June 1968. *John Cooper-Smith*

Above:

An impressive sight at Aller Junction in June 1969 as a blue/maroon pairing in the shape of No D822 *Hercules* and No D869 *Zest* rush by with train 1A64, the 15.20 Penzance–Paddington. The pair will have made light work of the South Devon banks, their combined power output being not far short of that produced by an IC125 High Speed Train unit. *Leslie Riley*

Right:

As already mentioned, when 'Warships' were working in multiple in accordance with their 'white diamond' code they were connected by a 36-pin jumper cable. However, when working the Royal Train special communications cables were employed between locomotives and stock. Seen at Oxford station on 2 May 1968 while on Royal Train duty (and with the cable clearly visible) are Nos D822 *Hercules* and D827 *Kelly. A. Whittaker*

Left:
In the early days of 'dieselisation' double-heading had little to do with fast timings and more to do with operational requirements. A single 'Warship' was restricted to just over 430 tons over the South Devon banks, but on 22 August 1959 the 8.35am Falmouth–Paddington loaded to 13 coaches and consequently required a pilot. Particularly fascinating is the pairing of the very first B-B 'Warship' with the very first 1,000hp 'Baby Warship', No D800 *Sir Brian Robertson* and No D6300 being seen approaching Dainton Summit. *J. R. Ainslie*

Left:
The infamous South Devon banks are about to be reduced to molehills as superpower is unleashed at Newton Abbot in 1969. Leaving the once-important railway centre are Nos D808 *Centaur* and 803 *Albion* with, according to the headcode, a down inter-regional working. The entire site has now been hugely rationalised and considerably reduced in status. *Ian Allan Library*

Left:
Just for a change, this photograph shows double-headed NBL 'D800' 'Warships' working in the county of Cornwall. Appropriately working the down 'Royal Duchy' on 7 September 1963 are Nos D858 *Valorous* and D848 *Sultan,* seen here approaching Liskeard station, junction for the Looe branch. The locomotives are working in tandem, with a footplate crew in each. *Maurice Dart collection*

Right:

Between 1958 and 1963 there were a few incursions by 'Warships' onto the Southern Region, but from September 1964 they took over all services between Waterloo and Exeter St Davids. By this time Southern steam was experiencing its 'last knockings', and under a complete reorganisation of West of England services steam withdrawals were continuing apace. A farewell steam-hauled 'East Devon Railtour' took place in February 1965, and a number of 'last steam train to Exeter' specials took place in 1966, by which time the 'Warships' were firmly established. A maroon No D869 *Zest* stands at Waterloo with the 16.00 for Exeter on 3 March 1968. *R. F. Roberts / SLS collection*

Right:

Word must have got around that the Class 42s were superior in terms of reliability and therefore availability to the Class 43s, and it seems the SR may have demanded that only Maybach-engined Class 42s should work the Waterloo–Exeter route. Certainly a failure in 'electricland' would have been catastrophic at peak periods. Gleaming at Waterloo on 22 May 1970 is No 816 *Eclipse* with the 17.00 departure for Exeter. *R. F. Roberts / SLS collection*

Right:

Passing beneath the Victoria–Clapham Junction line at Queens Road (now Queenstown Road), Battersea, on 9 January 1971 is No 811 *Daring* with the 12.30 from Exeter St Davids. The train had been diverted via the Windsor lines due to engineering work. *R. F. Roberts / SLS collection*

Above:

There is something special about London termini, and an experienced and artistically inclined photographer can secure great pictures. Oozing with atmosphere is this study of No 870 *Zulu* arriving at Waterloo from Exeter St Davids on 9 March 1971. As already mentioned, the 'D' (for 'diesel') number prefix was discontinued from the end of 1968, although some locomotives retained their original number long after that date. *John Cooper-Smith*

Left:

It seems amazing, with trains running 364 days a year, 24 hours a day, how few night photographs are taken by the railway fraternity. In this night scene from 25 September 1971 No 826 *Jupiter* has just come to rest at the Waterloo buffer-stops with the 16.00 from Exeter St Davids. Within a week there would be mass withdrawals of 'Warships' and services on the route would be taken over by the smaller 1,550hp Class 33 'Cromptons'.

R. F. Roberts / SLS collection

Right:

Another striking view of the Waterloo terminus during the last year of 'Warships' on the Exeter route, featuring No 803 *Albion* ready to leave with the 13.00 departure on 22 February 1971. Arriving (left) is Class 423 '4-VEP' electric unit No 7811; at the time of writing these too are about to be withdrawn from service, the last of the 'slam-door' electric multiple-units. *John Cooper-Smith*

Below:

In this very deceptive photograph No D817 *Foxhound* appears to be running through delightful countryside, but the location is in fact Clapham Cutting, in the South London suburbs! The train is the 12.00 Waterloo–Exeter/Sidmouth of 7 August 1965. The Sidmouth branch would close in March 1967. *J. Scrace*

Left:
No D816 *Eclipse* seems to have put in a colossal mileage on the Waterloo–Exeter route, judging by the number of photographs featuring the locomotive. Here the green machine hammers through Esher, station for Sandown Park racecourse, on 28 May 1966 with the 13.00 from Waterloo. *R. F. Roberts / SLS collection*

Left:
Another photograph at Esher, this time taken on 29 August 1964 … and the locomotive? No D816 *Eclipse!* The train is the 7.30am from Exeter Central, and behind the locomotive is an SR Bulleid BFK coach, a leftover from steam days. At this time the LSWR main line still had semaphore signals controlling train movements. *Ian Allan Library*

Left:
In days of old there was nothing more consistent with the image of an express train than a set of semaphore signals with two signals 'off' for the passing train. The upper-quadrant semaphores and the 'Warship' seen here had something in common — they were both doomed. Rushing through Walton-on-Thames on 5 May 1968 is the 15.00 from Waterloo to Exeter. *K. P. Lawrence*

Right:
In the days when the author had a very simple Ilford Sportsman camera with a maximum shutter speed of only 1/250sec action photography was not really an option. However, in January 1965, in place of the expected 'Merchant Navy' Pacific steam locomotive, a 'Warship' turned up at Weybridge on a Waterloo–Exeter working. At the time this was frequently enough to send one into the Shanty Café for a cuppa — how misguided we all were! — but at least on this occasion a 'snap' was taken. *John Vaughan*

Right:
Woking is where the line to Guildford and Portsmouth diverges from the Southampton/Salisbury route. Heading west from Woking on 13 July 1971 is maroon No D815 *Druid* at the head of the 13.08 from Waterloo. Within seven weeks the locomotive would be withdrawn, and the cutter's torch would ultimately eliminate a machine that had covered hundreds of thousands of miles in faithful service for BR. *J. Scrace*

Right:
When the 'Warships' were introduced in 1958 none of the freight trains on BR had air brakes, the options being vacuum-braked, partially fitted or loose-coupled. From the end of 1967 brake vans were no longer mandatory on fully fitted freight trains.
On loose-coupled workings the main criterion on many stretches of track was the holding power of a 20/25-ton brake van. The 'Warships' were capable performers on freight workings, such as this load of road stone for the construction of the M23 motorway, seen approaching Basingstoke on its way from Westbury to Merstham on 29 July 1972 behind No 829 *Magpie*. *John Faulkner*

Left:
The year 1966 was a bad one for the Waterloo–Exeter line, long sections of track between Wilton Junction, west of Salisbury, and Pinhoe, just east of Exmouth Junction, being singled in the interests of economy. This policy worked when every train was on time, but as soon as a train was late delays of at least 20 minutes could be incurred while a train in one direction waited in a passing loop for a late-running train in the opposite direction.
On 26 September 1966 No D829 *Magpie* enters Basingstoke from the west. *Gavin Morrison*

Above:
Sweeping off the non-electrified Salisbury line at Battledown flyover, west of Basingstoke, and joining the electrified Southampton route on 6 July 1967 is one of the original three Swindon-built 'Warships', No D802 *Formidable*, with a train from Exeter. The trio each had eight Laycock-Knorr cylinders, giving a braking force of 54 tons 16cwt, and were equipped with a passenger/goods valve that retarded normal brake applications when working fitted or partly fitted freights, to prevent wagon bunching. *J. L. McIvor*

Right:
Prior to the electrification of the Bournemouth line in 1967 'Warship' diesels sometimes worked to Southampton and Weymouth. On 12 September 1964 Maybach-engined No D813 *Diadem* was diagrammed for the 3.0pm Waterloo–Weymouth, seen passing SR 'Crompton' No D6541 on freight as it approaches Worting Junction, near Basingstoke. *Ron Fisher*

Right:
Andover Junction became just plain Andover once the line to Andover Town and Romsey closed in 1964. The old Midland & South Western Junction Railway line to Marlborough, Swindon and Cheltenham had previously closed to passengers in 1961, leaving the station as merely a junction for the freight line to Ludgershall. On 23 July 1969 No D805 *Benbow* leaves Andover with the 13.10 from Waterloo to Exeter St Davids. *J. Scrace*

Right:
From the end of 1964 passengers travelling from London to Exeter via the SR route would no longer get smuts of soot in their eyes or on their clothes from steam traction, but they might get a whiff of diesel fumes in Buckhorn Weston Tunnel! Seen departing Salisbury on 21 May 1965 is No D819 *Goliath* with the 13.00 from Waterloo. *R. F. Roberts / SLS collection*

Above:
One of the last 'Warships' to be painted in maroon livery was No D815 *Druid*. In this bright and crisp photograph train 6F11, comprising down empty Presflo cement wagons, possibly destined for Westbury, emerges from Fisherton Tunnel, Salisbury on 21 April 1967. A concrete bypass flyover has now spoiled this view. *G. F. Gillham*

Left:
Another photograph of No D815 *Druid* but this time taken at Wilton Junction, where the lines to Westbury, Bath and Bristol (left) leave the LSWR main line to Exeter. Taking the latter route is the 09.08 Waterloo–Exeter St Davids on 12 July 1970, this being the last full calendar year that the 'Warships' were in charge. *G. F. Gillham*

Right:
With the noble spire of Salisbury Cathedral visible above the rolling stock, blue-liveried Class 42 No 826 *Jupiter* unusually heads what the photographer describes as a special train for Cardiff away from the city and towards Wilton Junction. The date is 19 September 1971; on 18 October the locomotive was withdrawn from service — a fate shared that month by the remaining Class 43 fleet. *G. F. Gillham*

Below:
The rolling countryside around Buckhorn Weston Tunnel, between Gillingham in Dorset and Templecombe in Somerset, is extremely attractive. Climbing hard on the double track (since singled) is No D816 *Eclipse,* in green livery with small warning panel, with train 1V69, the 13.00 from Waterloo. *Ivo Peters*

Left:
Grossly overlooked on the old LSWR main line between Salisbury and Exeter were the local trains. Often in the 1960s these comprised WR diesel-mechanical units, but on occasions a 'Warship' would appear on these 'all stations' workings. Sunday 6 March 1966 was a dull, cold day, but the Spanner Mk 1a boiler on No D800 *Sir Brian Robertson* was in good shape, judging by the wisp of steam under the second coach. The Class 2 16.15 from Yeovil Town (not Junction!) to Waterloo is seen a train's length beyond Semley station, which closed officially and permanently from the following day. *Michael Mensing*

Left:
Back in April 1966 Yeovil Junction station had two wide island platforms, giving four platform faces, two through roads, numerous sidings and a marvellous pedestrian overbridge. The site would soon be rationalised! Leaving the station with an afternoon train is No D824 *Highflyer*. The service from Yeovil Junction to Yeovil Town ceased on 1 March 1967, and that to Yeovil Pen Mill on 6 May 1968. *L. A. Summers*

Right:
This 'Warship' profile was captured from the trackbed of the old Somerset & Dorset Joint Railway in July 1965. No D827 *Kelly* crosses the Bournemouth–Bath route with an up train, shortly after leaving Templecombe station's upper platform on the ex-LSWR main line; beneath the bridge is the small low-level platform. The S&D closed completely in March 1966, but the lower platform succumbed on 3 January that year. *John Vaughan*

Right:
Although there was (and still is!) a village adjacent to the Templecombe station area the station's primary purpose was to provide a link with the north–south axis of the Somerset & Dorset Joint Railway. Consequently when the S&D, from 7 March 1966, so too did Templecombe station. However, there was a happy ending to the story when, decades later, as a result of the efforts of a local pressure group, the station reopened. On the weekend of closure in 1966 No D818 *Glory* arrives with an express for Waterloo. *Gavin Morrison*

Above:
Exeter Central was traditionally the SR's station in the city, whereas Exeter St Davids was GWR territory. However, in order to gain access to its North Devon and Cornwall lines the SR had running rights between Exeter St Davids and Cowley Bridge Junction. Following Nationalisation in 1948 rivalries diminished, and by the early 1960s the WR operated all lines in Devon and Cornwall. Coming off the former Southern lines at Cowley Bridge in 1967 is No 813 *Diadem* with a fitted ballast train from Meldon Quarry. *John Cooper-Smith*

Above:
Photographs of 'Warships' at former LSWR intermediate stations between Barnstaple and Ilfracombe are hard to come by. In this interesting view a Summer Saturday Ilfracombe–Waterloo express is double-headed by a 'Baby Warship' and a Swindon-built 'D800'. The train is seen arriving at Morthoe & Woolacombe, the summit of the line, with more passengers waiting to board. *J. R. Ball*

Right:
Somewhat away from the Ilfracombe line but an interesting Devon working on SR lines is this view of the up 'Cornish Riviera Express' approaching Meldon Junction, near Okehampton, on 26 August 1961. No D867 *Zenith* had been diverted via the SR route due to engineering work on the WR main line; the formation would have reversed at Plymouth North Road. The line between Meldon and Bere Alston would close in 1968, the alternative Plymouth–Exeter route being eliminated at a stroke. *S. C. Nash*

Above:
The North Devon terminus of Ilfracombe was something of an outpost of the SR West Country network. Although traffic was always seasonal, under WR ownership the service declined, and in October 1970 the line closed completely, becoming part of the SR's 'Withered Arm'. Arriving at Ilfracombe on 10 August 1968 with the 07.35 from Newton Abbot is No D820 *Grenville*. *M. Edwards*

Left:
In February 1959 the 'Warships' were introduced on the 'Bristolian', with a Bristol–Paddington average speed of 70mph. Although the 'Warships' worked Paddington–Plymouth/Penzance services for most of their working lives the 2,200hp B-Bs also worked Bristol expresses almost exclusively for their first four years of service. Even after the introduction of the 'Westerns' and the arrival of Brush Type 4s 'Warships' could still be found on Bristol trains and remained thus until the late 1960s. No D851 *Temeraire* is seen passing Scours Lane sidings, on the approach to Reading, with the 11.35 Weston-super-Mare–Paddington. *Gerald T. Robinson*

Reading–Bristol

Above:
As the years went by and larger and more powerful Type 4 locomotives arrived on the WR some 'Warships' were replaced on Class 1 passenger trains and cascaded to a wide variety of freight workings. There has always been plenty of freight traffic between Reading and Didcot, and on 29 October 1968 No D859 *Vanquisher* is seen heading a lengthy down freight near Tilehurst. *John Cooper-Smith*

Right:
In trials in 1958 between Bristol and Didcot No D801 was tested rigorously on trains loading to 15 coaches. With a lighter load the highest speed downhill on maximum power was 103mph. On the inaugural down run of the 'Bristolian' on 15 June 1959 No D804 *Avenger* travelled from Paddington to Bristol Temple Meads via the 117.6-mile Badminton route in 92min 52sec, and speeds of 100-102mph were attained on three occasions, admittedly with a modest (260-ton) trailing load. On 22 September 1961 No D831 *Monarch* was travelling only slightly slower on the down fast line at Moreton, east of Didcot, with the 4.45pm Paddington–Bristol.
Michael Mensing

Left:
For reasons unknown two 'Warship' locomotives, Nos D845 *Sprightly* and D858 *Valorous,* received small yellow cab-end warning panels that were considerably smaller in area than normal. On a glorious 22 September 1961 *Sprightly* rushes past Milton, west of Didcot, with the 10.35am Weston-super-Mare–Paddington. Note also the unusual yellow band above the cab windows.
Michael Mensing

Left:
With a delightful rake of older rolling stock behind it, No D815 *Druid,* in original livery, takes to the up slow line at Moreton, east of Didcot, with the 2A20 4.18pm Swindon–Paddington on 22 September 1961 — seemingly a good day for 'Warships' in the area.
Michael Mensing

Left:
In the days when one could almost guarantee a group of trainspotters on any important railway platform and when an Ian Allan 'ABC' could be one's most valuable possession, much interest is shown in No 824 *Highflyer* pausing at Swindon with an up Class 8 freight on 21 November 1970. *R. F. Roberts / SLS collection*

Centre left:
The original 117-ton A1A-A1A 'Warship', No D600 *Active*, first arrived at Swindon in January 1958. There it underwent familiarisation and shakedown trials to Gloucester and back, followed in March by a trip to Plymouth. This shot shows the locomotive at Swindon on 9 March 1958. The original 'Warships' could work in multiple with the first six 1,000hp 'Baby Warships' (Nos D6300-5), because they shared the 'orange square' coupling code, but not with the later 1,100hp (D6306 *et seq*) locomotives. *R. A. Panting*

Below:
Another fascinating view recorded at Swindon more than 45 years ago, featuring an almost-new No D801 *Vanguard* at the business end of the 4.15pm from Paddington to Plymouth via Bristol on Saturday 8 August 1958. At this time the diesels were 'new fangled', and although they turned plenty of heads the majority of enthusiasts spurned them because they heralded the death of the steam locomotive. *R. F. Roberts/SLS collection*

Left:
Another view of Swindon, which, in terms of construction of the Maybach-engined fleet, all heavy overhauls and, for many locomotives, final scrapping, was the home of the 'Warships'. This photograph, taken with the special permission of British Rail Engineering, has been included because it was taken from a high elevation above the roof of the works building near the old pattern shop. Fortunately the 16-cylinder Maybach-engined Class 35 diesel-hydraulic 'Hymek' No D7029 (in the foreground) and No D821 *Greyhound* (furthest from the camera) were preserved, but, as mentioned earlier, No 818 *Glory* was cut up.
John Vaughan

Right:
Whenever a brand-new 'Warship' emerged from or was delivered to Swindon it was despatched on a test run (or 'shakedown', in modern parlance), an elderly rake of stock often being summoned merely to provide a suitable load test for the locomotive and its components. On its very first run No D809 *Champion* rattles through Bathampton, to the east of Bath, with a test run from Swindon in August 1959.
Ian Allan Library

Right:
On Sunday 9 February 1969 the Berks & Hants line was closed for engineering work, and consequently West Country trains were all diverted via Swindon and Bath. Crossing the River Avon at Bathford is the diverted down 'Cornish Riviera Express' behind the (by then) customary pair of 'Warships', No D803 *Albion* leading.
John C. Saltwell

Above:
From the autumn of 1965 overhauled 'Warships' were outshopped in maroon livery. However, fewer than half the class were so treated, because from the beginning of 1967 BR corporate blue became standard, and Swindon was obliged to comply. Its maroon livery looking tired, No D828 *Magnificent* approaches Keynsham with the 11.15 Bristol–Paddington express on 6 April 1968. *P. J. Fowler*

Left:
In July 1959, in superb evening light, an immaculate No D805 *Benbow,* recently delivered in green livery, sweeps towards Sydney Gardens in Bath with the 4.15pm Paddington–Plymouth, its '443' headcode belonging to the steam age. Only 26 examples would go through the full green/maroon/blue cycle before withdrawal. This locomotive would be one of the last 10 'Warships' in service, being withdrawn on 24 October 1972. *Ian Allan Library*

Above:
Eight years after the previous photograph was taken No D805 *Benbow* was still hard at work on the Bristol road, this time in adverse climatic conditions. The locomotive is seen leaving St Annes Park Tunnel and approaching the now closed station on 8 December 1967 with the 09.45 Paddington–Weston-super-Mare, running about half an hour late. St Annes Park station would close in 1970. *P. J. Fowler*

Right:
The Mendip stone of Bath's fine terraces stands out in the afternoon sunshine as No 847 *Strongbow* rounds the curve into Bath Spa on 29 April 1970 with a breakdown train which is most definitely *not* the 1A06! Most unusually the BR double-arrow logo is placed above the nameplate. *John Cooper-Smith*

Above:
An absolutely charming study at the down end of Bristol Temple Meads as a father and son admire a brand-new No D810 *Cockade,* standing proudly at the head of the 'Devonian' on 28 September 1959. The headcode discs display the 'express passenger' headcode. The water crane on the left would be in use for another five years, until 'dieselisation' was complete. *Michael Mensing*

Left:
It may seem strange to some that a 78-ton 'Warship' should have been chosen for the publicity shots for a new WR freight flow. On the inaugural run of a weekly BOCM freight working of animal and poultry foods from the docks at Avonmouth, near Bristol, to Cornwall No D838 *Rapid* pulls out of snow-covered sidings at Avonmouth on 13 January 1963. *Ian Allan Library*

South Wales

Above:
Although 'Warships' worked into Newport on trains via the North & West route from 1962, the original A1A-A1A locomotives made a brief appearance on coal trains in 1967, and various B-B examples worked freight 'across the border', over the years the 'Warship' classes were not the most common type of diesel locomotive in Wales. Nevertheless, in April 1970 Nos 803-6/36/57/61/7 were all noted in the Cardiff area on coal trains. A year later, on 22 April 1971, No 857 *Undaunted* emerges from Newport Tunnel and enters the station with the 16.00 Margam–East Usk Junction coal empties. *David Wharton*

Right:
Ironically South Wales was to be the graveyard and the final resting place for many 'Warships', but in happier times these locomotives worked trains of animal feedstuffs and flour for Cornwall from Barry Docks as well as Avonmouth. Here an unidentified locomotive heads a long train of vacuum-braked four-wheelers running as a Class 5 freight, the train reputedly including 10,000 bags of flour. This area is now virtually devoid of freight traffic, and the docks belong to the scenes of yesteryear. *Ian Allan Library*

Left:
From the start of 'dieselisation' a great variety of motive power has been used on the Oxford–Worcester line, and over the years services between Paddington and Worcester/Hereford have been worked by Classes 31, 35, 42, 43, 47, 50 and 52. 'Warships' were working services on the line by 1964, and it was noted in March 1968 that No D855 was crew training between Paddington, Worcester and Hereford. Between 1968 and 1970 Class 42 and 43 locomotives were regular performers, but on 29 December 1971 No 818 was recorded as being 'unusually' noted. Here No 858 *Valorous* passes Bruern Crossing with the 16.15 Worcester–Paddington on 7 March 1970. *Bryan Hicks*

The Worcester Road

Left:
With the delightful Cotswold village of Aston Magna in the background No 833 *Panther* runs between Moreton-in-Marsh and Chipping Campden with the 1F33 express from Paddington on 16 May 1970. The Class 35 'Hymeks' had a long stint on the line and were normally in charge of the half a dozen trains per day that by then ran between London and Worcester (four of these continuing to Hereford), thereby maintaining the route's association with diesel-hydraulic locomotives. *Bryan Hicks*

Left:
With a dusting of snow on the Gloucestershire countryside No 833 *Panther* passes the site of the erstwhile Adlestrop station (closed from January 1966) on the afternoon of 7 March 1970 with a train from Worcester to Paddington. The one-time stationmaster's house is on the left. *Bryan Hicks*

Right:
In the early days of 'dieselisation' 'Warships' regularly worked between Paddington, Birmingham, Wolverhampton, Shrewsbury and Birkenhead, using mostly the 'Birmingham Direct' route via Princes Risborough. However, once the LMR West Coast main line was electrified in the mid-1960s the old GWR route became secondary in terms of London traffic. There were still through trains from Paddington to Birmingham, but these were mainly in the hands of 'Westerns' and Brush Type 4s, and the majority travelled via Oxford. However, in October 1967 15 of the latter type were transferred to other regions to cover shortfalls, and a similar number of 'Warships' were drafted in to cover the diagrams. Seen passing Cape Road goods yard at Warwick on 13 October 1967 is maroon No D844 *Spartan* with a Paddington–Birmingham New Street express. *Bryan Hicks*

Right:
The rain has stopped and the sun has come out as the wet platforms of Leamington Spa station reflect the upper-quadrant semaphore signals on 11 November 1967. Arriving from Birmingham New Street at 09.15 with a train diverted to Marylebone is No D846 *Steadfast*. All of the transferred-in 'Warships' on the WR Birmingham line were maintained at Old Oak Common. For further views on this route see page 55. *Bryan Hicks*

Above:
'Warship' locomotives were regularly used on Royal trains, even though there were at times question marks about the reliability of the locomotives. As a small sample, No D819 *Goliath* worked a Royal Train from Windsor to Southampton Western Docks on 7 August 1967, Nos D827 and D822 transported HM The Queen to Oxford on 2 May 1968, and on 7 March 1971 No D821 *Greyhound* worked the very last train (a Royal Train) through the SR Devonport Kings Road station at Plymouth. In this 1969 view No 816 *Eclipse* rounds the curve at Aller Junction with a full 11-coach Torquay–Exeter Royal Train working. *Ian Allan Library*

Royal Duty

Left:
As late as 1971 the WR and SR were still prepared to roster 'Warships' for Royal Train duties, albeit working singly. On 10 November 1971 No 818 *Glory* transported Royalty from Exeter to Barnstaple, and in this November 1971 view a Class 42 'Warship' was a surprise visitor to Victoria station in London. Such workings were normally to Gatwick or to Tattenham Corner in conjunction with the running of the Derby horse race on Epsom Downs. *Ian Allan Library*

Right:
Although the 'Warships' were WR locomotives, between 1964 and 1971 they worked the majority of Waterloo–Exeter services over mostly SR lines. The class also regularly visited other parts of the SR, especially the South Western and Central divisions. One of the freight flows that often produced a 'Warship' was the Eastleigh–Chichester goods. On 25 October 1966 a maroon Swindon-built example is seen in the up side down bay platform at the West Sussex county town. A supermarket now covers the cattle pen and sidings on the right, although a new aggregate freight flow commenced during 2004.
John Vaughan

Right:
When the Class 52 'Westerns', Class 55 'Deltics' and Class 40 'Whistlers' were about to be withdrawn there were dozens of farewell specials, but in respect of the 'Warships' and the 'Hymeks' diesel-locomotive enthusiasm was in its infancy, and the number of fans was small compared to the legions of fanatical followers of the aforementioned classes. Nevertheless, there *were* a handful of specials, and one such train enterprisingly took members of the Plymouth Railway Circle from Plymouth to Haywards Heath for a visit to the Bluebell Railway. Seen approaching the author's home station of Goring-by-Sea in West Sussex on 16 April 1972 is No 810 *Cockade* with the outward journey of train 1Z64. *John Vaughan*

Left:
When the M23 and M25 motorways were being built a vast quantity of road stone was required, and a site was established at Merstham, near Redhill, in Surrey. The stone came mostly from Somerset quarries, and this resulted in daily 'Warship' visits to the Southern. No 807 *Caradoc* is seen passing Guildford station, returning empties from Merstham to Westbury, on 16 June 1972. *R. E. Ruffell*

Right:
These stone empties were photographed from a moving train in the days when doors slammed and windows opened. However, it was not a practice that could be recommended and was not without risk! In 1972 there were still 13 'Warships', working their last summer, one of which, No 805 *Benbow*, is seen at Woking with empty stone hoppers on 7 September. *R. E. Ruffell*

Left:
It is obvious from these scenes that over the years No D805 was a regular performer on freight trains. An earlier photograph, taken on 24 September 1966, with the locomotive carrying the 'D' prefix and in maroon livery, shows *Benbow* at Romsey with a Class 6 fitted freight from the WR to Eastleigh. *R. F. Roberts / SLS collection*

Left:
During the 1960s the BR Board had labelled diesel-hydraulics non-standard, and by the early 1970s it was clear that the 'Warships' were not going to be around for long. This provided the impetus for many enthusiasts to go out and find the few remaining 'Warships' before they became extinct. In this August 1972 view, recorded at the down end of the Salisbury station site, No 818 *Glory* departs with yet more stone wagon empties, bound initially for Westbury. *John Vaughan*

Right:
On occasions 'Warships' disgraced themselves, but with rostered annual mileages of between 70,000 and 90,000 (less by the 1970s) failures were inevitable. In July 1972 No 824 *Highflyer* failed at Merstham on one of the motorway-construction stone trains from Westbury and had to be rescued by Class 33 'Crompton' No 6585 (later No 33 065). Repairs would be carried out back on the WR, the locomotive continuing in service until 3 December 1972. *John Vaughan*

Right:
A regular flow of stone and aggregates that is still thriving is that from the Somerset quarries of Merehead and Whatley to Fareham, in Hampshire. Nowadays modern high-tech General Motors locomotives haul 100-ton wagons to the unloading siding, but in July 1972 it was a Class 42 and old vacuum-braked hoppers that invaded the SR. No 820 *Grenville* was photographed behind Fareham West signalbox before returning to Westbury. By this time the locomotive had just 16 weeks to 'live'. *John Vaughan*

Above:
This cracking view shows the unique Paxman-engined 'Warship' No D830 *Majestic*. The Paxman engines were marginally more powerful than either the MAN or Maybach engines but were also slightly longer, and some redesign was necessary to accommodate them within the standard structure; on reflection it is perhaps surprising that the locomotive didn't have its own sub-class. On Sunday 4 June 1967 the locomotive was photographed at the head of a 10-coach Weymouth-bound excursion train near the closed Monkton & Came (Golf Links) Halt, south of Dorchester. *Michael Mensing*

Left:
This fascinating picture was taken at Butts Junction, near Alton, on Sunday 5 June 1966 and shows No D814 *Dragon* descending from Medstead & Four Marks with the diverted 07.19 Eastleigh–Waterloo. The line on the left ran down to Farringdon, once the first halt on the old Meon Valley line, while in the distance and diverging to the right is the siding to Treloar Hospital which once formed part of the old Basingstoke & Alton Light Railway. *C. Small*

Exeter–Penzance

Above:
The line from Exeter to Penzance is arguably the most scenic and operationally the most exciting on the WR. The 131½-mile route includes the run beside the sea on the South Devon coast, the formidable South Devon banks on the southern fringe of Dartmoor, the magnificent Tamar Estuary, innumerable Cornish viaducts traversing deep, wooded valleys, passing distant china-clay tips and through an old mining area and extensive farmland before ending at the buffer-stops at Penzance, by the delightful Mounts Bay, in Cornwall. However, the passengers on this train at Exeter St Davids will not experience the run because they are heading for London Waterloo! No D817 *Foxhound*, in maroon livery, prepares to leave with the 10.15 departure on 22 May 1971. *N. E. Preedy*

Right:
It is high summer at Dawlish, and every bench seat along the promenade is occupied, the stretch of sand near Dawlish station being particularly packed with sunbathers and swimmers. Passing the busy scene is the 12-coach 1C35 from Paddington, headed by an unidentified 'Warship', on 25 July 1962. *A. P. Crane*

Above:

It seems that by 1 September 1972 the practice of arm-waving or 'flailing' from train windows by ardent supporters of a particular class was already established! Branded by many as juvenile behaviour, much energy would be exerted in this way over the following decades as class after class of diesel locomotive became extinct. No 818 *Glory* was definitely not working train 6B21 as it picked up speed near Teignmouth with an up express. *Gavin Morrison*

Left:
Some of the rolling stock in this scene from the early days of dieselisation looks dated, even by 1950s standards. Leaving Newton Abbot for the Midlands with a modest load of six coaches is No D824 *Highflyer*. The arrival of the 'Warships' resulted in significant changes to locomotive diagramming, because a single locomotive could work from Paddington to Penzance and back in a single day — a feat that no steam locomotive could emulate. Such availability meant that far fewer diesel locomotives would be required than their steam counterparts.
Ian Allan Library

Right:
Another very early photograph of a 'Warship' in action in the 1950s is this view along the banks of the River Teign on 11 October 1959. No D805 *Benbow* is at the head of the 'Cornish Riviera Express', comprising 12 coaches. Had a steam locomotive been in charge, assistance would have been required from Newton Abbot. From the early 1960s the 'Rivo' included a portion for the Torbay line, which was detached at Newton Abbot. *D. S. Fish*

Below:
When photographed on 14 July 1969 No 804 *Avenger* had just been repainted in blue livery with BR double-arrows beneath each cab window. The two Maybach engines would be on full power through Aller Junction in readiness for the climb through Stoneycombe to Dainton Summit with the heavy 12-coach 'Cornishman', train 1V70. *G. F. Gillham*

Left:
Another immaculate blue-liveried 'Warship' leaving Newton Abbot, but this time a Class 43 and with a single BR double-arrow located below the nameplate. With the cooling tower of the long-since-demolished power station in the background, No 852 *Tenacious* departs with the 11.20 Paddington–Penzance on 27 July 1976. *Leslie Riley*

Below left:
Although running a pair of 'Warships' on crack express trains was more expensive than running a single 2,700hp locomotive, nothing rivalled a pair of Class 42s for power until the arrival of IC125 High Speed Train units in the West Country in 1979. When single Class 47 or Class 52 locomotives worked such trains as the 'Cornish Riviera Express' in this era either timings had to be relaxed or train loads reduced. Nos D803 *Albion* and D822 *Hercules* make light work of the 08.30 Plymouth–Paddington at Dainton on 25 April 1968. *C. H. S. Owen*

Above right:
The track layout and station infrastructure at Newton Abbot have been much rationalised since this 1962 view was recorded. All of the lines on the right have been removed, and the semaphore signals have long gone, as have the water columns seen either side of 'Warship' No D806 *Cambrian*, in charge of the 3.0pm Plymouth–Cardiff on 25 July 1962. *D. Ian Wood*

Right:
A down Chartex or Adex special train threads the hills of South Devon while descending from Dainton Summit on 6 August 1971 behind No 825 *Intrepid*. From May 1969 'Warships' had a classification panel applied under the number on the cab ends, giving data regarding locomotive weight, route availability and maximum speed. *John Cooper-Smith*

Above:
At the end of 1969 it was announced that maintenance expenditure on all Class 43 'Warships' would be reduced and full works overhauls eliminated, although it would be some time before the more cost-effective Class 42s were similarly treated. With Brent Knoll in the background (right), No D866 *Zebra* heads train 1C49, the 08.35 Manchester Piccadilly–Plymouth, between South Brent and Wrangaton on 18 July 1970. *John M. Boyes*

Left:
Totnes was once an important point on the South Devon main line; as well as being the junction for the Ashburton branch it saw significant milk traffic from the nearby dairy and had a thriving goods yard. With a rake of six-wheeled 3,000gal milk tankers in the sidings and a couple of milk lorries visible in the station yard No D822 *Hercules* arrives at the up platform with the 13.55 Plymouth–Leeds on 17 July 1970. *G. F. Gillham*

Above:
Until the Kingsbridge branch closed on 16 September 1963 passengers changed trains at the junction station of Brent, the latter surviving until 5 October 1964. In happier times, on 28 July 1962, a very clean No D864 *Zambesi* pauses with the 7.30am Penzance–Paddington. The branch DMU can be seen on the far left. D. *Ian Wood*

Right:
The extensive rebuilding of Plymouth North Road station began in 1956 but was not completed until June 1962! In the early months of 1958 the first two 117-ton NBL 'Warships' could often be found working either the 'Cornish Riviera Express' or the 'Royal Duchy'. On this occasion No D600 *Active,* on the down 'CRE', must have been running hot, being seen (somewhat amusingly) taking water from a steam-locomotive water crane! *P. Q. Treloar*

Right:
It is entirely appropriate that a photograph of a West Country milk train should be included in *The Power of the Warships*, because sometimes loadings were such that plenty of power was needed to haul the 3,000gal tankers over the Cornish and Devon banks. Depending on the era, major loading-points on the main line were St Erth, Dalcoath, Lostwithiel, Saltash and Totnes, with feeders from such places as Hemyock and Torrington. On 27 August 1971 No 814 *Dragon*, with an up load, waits for a crew change at Plymouth North Road. Such traffic would be lost to road transport from 1980. *John Cooper-Smith*

Above:
Curving off the classic 1859 Royal Albert Bridge at the mandatory 15mph speed limit and entering Saltash station on 8 June 1970 is No 829 *Magpie* with the 17.10 Plymouth–Penzance commuter train. The single-track bridge was designed by Isambard Kingdom Brunel and spans not only the River Tamar but also the border between Devon and Cornwall. *R. F. Roberts / SLS collection*

Right:

In 2004 Liskeard station was completely redeveloped, but in this 1970 view it still had in place an ugly brick extension which contrasted with the lovely original Cornwall Railway building at street level. The station is located in a cutting and is also the junction for Moorswater and the Looe branch. On 22 July a Class 7 freight with a payload of bagged and powdered china clay climbs through the station behind No D842 *Royal Oak. G. F. Gillham*

Below:

The stretch of line through the Glynn Valley, between Doublebois and Bodmin Road, is one of the finest in the country; twisting and turning around the hillsides that overlook the River Fowey, it abounds with impressive viaducts, while gradients are as steep as 1 in 57. No D816 *Eclipse* will be on notch 7 as it heads up the valley with the 11.30 Penzance–Paddington on 26 April 1962. The locomotive and leading coaches are covered by cloud, but just behind Penadlake Viaduct the weather is sunny. *J. C. Beckett*

Left:
Throughout their working lives all three classes of 'Warship' were regular performers in the county of Cornwall, on all types of train. Seen at Bodmin Road in July 1963, No D858 *Valorous* interestingly has a steam-age metal '83D' (Plymouth Laira) shedcode disc on the buffer-beam. The station was the junction for Bodmin General and Wadebridge, which branch closed to passengers on 30 January 1967. The Bodmin & Wenford Railway now runs over part of the line, which has resulted in the line's being preserved for posterity.
Alan Bryant

Left:
In workaday condition Class 42 No D867 *Zenith* shows the ultimate in versatility by hauling a rake of small four-wheeled vacuum-braked china-clay wagons out of the down loop at Lostwithiel on Monday 8 June 1970. The paint on the bodywork of the 'Warships' was gradually damaged by the chemicals in the water of washing plants, giving many locomotives a particularly run-down appearance.
R. F. Roberts / SLS collection

Left:
Until early in 2004 Cornwall was always a mecca for parcels-, van- and postal-train workings. Trains left Penzance for Paddington, Bristol Temple Meads, Glasgow, Willesden and even Redhill, in Surrey. The stock was always truly mixed, some vehicles pre-dating the 1948 Nationalisation. At the head of a train of vans, with LMR example No M31231M leading, is No D805 *Benbow*, seen at St Austell on 8 June 1970.
R. F. Roberts / SLS collection

Right:
Leaving the Cornish main line at Par, the Newquay branch was an important stamping-ground for the 'Warships' because it retained the traditional through holiday-train facility in the summer months, thousands of holidaymakers being conveyed from the UK's major cities to the Cornish seaside in full-length trains. At such times 'Warships' could be seen in abundance, especially on Saturdays. On 20 June 1970 No D831 *Monarch* waits to leave Newquay, while the local DMU can be seen on the right. *John Vaughan*

Right:
Photographs of Swindon-built 'Warships' on local stopping trains between Par and Newquay are quite rare. On Saturday 15 July 1961 No D816 *Eclipse* was diagrammed to work the 10.5am Par–Newquay, which comprised three non-corridor coaches and is seen near Tolcarn Junction. The steam-hauled 11.0 departure for York can just be seen behind the last coach of the local. *R. S. Clare*

Right:
Rolling down the hill into Par station is No D800 *Sir Brian Robertson* with the up 'Cornish Riviera Express' in 1958. Note the huge water tank on the right and the signals on the spur to St Blazey Yard. During its 10 years of service this locomotive would cover some 927,000 miles; withdrawn in October 1968, it would be the only B-B 'Warship' to go for scrap still in green livery. *Author's collection*

Above:
The single white disc just below the windscreen makes a change from the usual express-passenger headcode featured in many other early views and indicates that this is a local or Class 2 train, in fact the 9.15am Penzance–Plymouth, seen arriving at Truro on Whit Monday (18 May) 1959 behind No D802 *Formidable*. On the right is the yard shunter and station pilot, No D3509. *Michael Mensing*

Below:
The first three B-B 'Warships' were ordered in January 1956, and from the drawing board to completion each took 2½ years. The drawing-office effort alone amounted to 75,000 hours, such was the task of adapting the major components to fit the UK loading gauge, although the origins of the 'D800s' remained undeniably German. No D800 *Sir Brian Robertson* is framed by the awning of Truro station while heading the up 'CRE' on 12 May 1959. *Michael Mensing*

Right:
A telephoto lens provides plenty of impact of the 'Warship'-hauled 11.05 Penzance–Paddington of 29 August 1970, crossing what is believed to be Tregagle Viaduct, east of Truro. Within two years more powerful Class 52 diesel-hydraulics and Class 47 diesel-electrics would work all such trains, and by 1975 BR's final diesel-electric passenger (in reality mixed-traffic) locomotive design, the Class 50, would be in charge. *Michael H. C. Baker*

Above:
Having already featured Nos D800 and D802 opposite, here we feature the third of the original trio of B-B 'Warships', No D801 *Vanguard,* passing the steam shed at Truro c1959. Soon the arrival of further diesel-hydraulic locomotives would make serious inroads into the number of steam locomotives in service. The original aim of the Modernisation Plan — complete 'dieselisation' of all services west of Newton Abbot — would be achieved in a little over five years. No D801 would be the very first B-B 'Warship' to be withdrawn, on 3 August 1968 — a working life of less than 10 years.
P. Q. Treloar

Left:
As time went on it was more difficult to obtain spares from NBL, and the original A1A-A1A 'Warships' could be out of service for some time. Under pressure to reduce the number of classes, BR withdrew all five in December 1967, the locomotives being placed in store at Laira. Back in its halcyon days No D601 *Ark Royal* is seen crossing Angarrack Viaduct with the up 'CRE' on 26 July 1958. *P. Q. Treloar*

Left:
No D813 was the first 'Warship' to be fitted with roller-blind headcode panels, but it would appear from this photograph that either the blind is not working or the driver is not familiar with its operation. Passing Marazion station on 7 April 1960, No D813 *Diadem* heads the 11.0am Penzance–Paddington, alias the 'Royal Duchy'. In common with many other intermediate Cornish stations, Marazion would close with effect from 5 October 1964. *P. Q. Treloar*

Left:
St Erth was and still is the junction station for the St Ives branch. However, it is no longer a major centre for milk distribution by rail, and a 'Warship' has not passed through the station for well over 30 years. On Thursday 4 June 1970 blue-liveried No 854 *Tiger* waits to depart with the up milk, having just reversed onto the up main line from the adjacent sidings. The track between the locomotive and the signalbox is also the lead onto the St Ives branch.
R. F. Roberts / SLS collection

Above:
This view of the railway line at Penzance gives a good appreciation of the juxtaposition of the terminus (distant left), the town (centre) and Mounts Bay (left). Large granite rocks protect the railway from high tides and stormy seas. In days gone by the railway was regularly washed away, and despite the rock protection in October 2004 the line was again damaged. Getting to grips with the up 'Cornish Riviera Express' on 23 September 1959 is No D800 *Sir Brian Robertson. P. Q. Treloar*

Left:
The end of the line at Penzance, just over 305 miles from London via the Berks & Hants cut-off route, on 13 May 1961 finds No D813 *Diadem* at the business end of a departing up 'Royal Duchy'. The five original 'Warships' were withdrawn in 1967, three Class 42s went in 1968, and four more B-Bs in 1969. The year 1970 was withdrawal-free, but no fewer than 45 'Warships' were taken out of service in 1971, including all of the remaining Class 43s; the surviving 19 Class 42s had all gone by the end of 1972. Fortunately two Class 42s survived the cutter's torch, and the following plates show the class in preservation. *Cecil J. Blay*

Left:
Although the first B-B 'Warship' to be withdrawn was No D801 in August 1968, the locomotive with the shortest working life was No D840 *Resistance,* which lasted only eight years, from February 1961 until April 1969. The highest-mileage Class 43 was No D858 *Valorous,* with 801,000 miles on the clock, whereas certain Class 42s exceeded the magic 1 million-mile total. The very last 'Warship' to be removed from the BR stocklists was No D832 *Onslaught* on 16 December 1972, but on 10 January 1973 the locomotive travelled under its own power to the Derby Technical Centre for possible further experimental use. It was eventually sold for preservation and after a long restoration process is seen leaving Brooksbottom Tunnel, on the East Lancashire Railway, with the 11.15 departure from Bury on 8 June 1996. *Gavin Morrison*

Preserved Warships

Left:
Looking particularly smart in black livery with small yellow warning panel, No D832 *Onslaught* arrives at Rawtenstall from Bury on 5 March 1994. The line, which once continued beyond Rawtenstall to Bacup, closed to passengers on 5 December 1966 and was reopened in stages, starting in 1987. *Gavin Morrison*

Right:
In BR service only two 'Warships' appeared in BR blue livery with a small yellow warning panel, these being Nos D830 *Majestic* and D831 *Monarch*. However, such a sight was recreated on the East Lancashire Railway in 1993 as seen in this well-executed shot. Making a dramatic appearance near Burrs, No D821 *Greyhound* in blue and No D832 *Onslaught* in black livery power through the Lancashire countryside on Saturday 2 October 1993. *Gavin Morrison*

Right:
Another progressive preserved line to support diesel traction is the North Yorkshire Moors Railway, which runs from Grosmont to Pickering. The first 'Warship' to be used in preservation, in 1987, No D821 *Greyhound* was photographed in maroon livery just a year later, on 23 April 1988, passing some magnificent scenery at Darnholme in North Yorkshire while climbing to Goathland with a train for Pickering. *Gavin Morrison*

Right:
Three years later the owners of No D821 *Greyhound* repainted it in blue livery. Looking magnificent on 27 April 1991, the locomotive approaches Deviation Curve *en route* to Pickering, the sound of the 'Maybach organs' reverberating off the North Yorkshire hillsides. It would appear the track has also been upgraded; presumably there are some sleepers below the ballast! *Gavin Morrison*

Left:

One of the joys of today's preservation scene is the transfer of locomotives from one line to another, either on long-term loan or simply for diesel weekends, providing the enthusiast and the photographer with a whole range of new possibilities. On 1 October 1995 No 832 *Onslaught* was busy on the West Somerset Railway with a train bound for Minehead. The lovely semaphore signal is just below the A39 road at Williton. *P. G. Barnes*

Below:

The miserable 'British summer' weather is not dampening spirits in this lively scene at Bishops Lydeard on 17 May 1997. The branch line from Taunton to Minehead closed on 4 January 1971, but the preservationists later moved in to try and save the line. Fortunately they were successful, although problems concerning regular access to the junction station of Taunton remain. The line once had through locomotive-hauled holiday trains to Minehead, where there is a large holiday camp. Recalling those days is this excellent shot of No D821 *Greyhound* waiting for the road to Minehead. *Gavin Morrison*

Right:
On 29 October 1994 the West Somerset Railway held a rather grand diesel gala. A sight to send diesel-hydraulic fans wild was a Class 42/Class 52 pairing, seen at Williton apparently heading the 'Torbay Express'! A total of 48 Maybach cylinders are opened up as 'Warship' No 821 *Greyhound* and 'Western' No D1035 *Western Yeoman* (alias D1010) head for Bishops Lydeard. The Maybach cylinder heads had a reputation for cracking, but one hopes that on this occasion all remained intact. *P. G. Barnes*

Centre right:
Already featured in both blue and maroon liveries, No D821 *Greyhound* is seen here resplendent in original green livery but with small yellow warning panel. The Mid-Hants Railway (or Watercress Line) is another to take an enlightened view of diesel traction, and there was plenty of internal-combustion-engined power at its 'Trainspotters' Ball 2' on 8 April 2001. The 'Warship' double-headed Class 20 No 20 188 on the 13.25 Alresford–Alton, the pair being seen leaving Medstead & Four Marks station. *P. G. Barnes*

Below right:
An eye-opener for the blinkered 'steam-only' preserved lines is this shot at Medstead & Four Marks, also taken on 8 April 2001. The trains and platforms are wedged with modern-traction fans as the 12.06 Alton–Alresford arrives at Medstead behind No D821 Greyhound and passes the 11.55 Alresford–Alton, hauled by Class 50 No D449 *Defiance* and Class 37 No 37 308. The task of preserving a diesel locomotive should not be underestimated, requiring as it does a significant degree of electrical-engineering knowledge as well as the largely mechanical knowledge necessitated by other preservation projects. The author trusts that the preservationists of the important WR diesel-hydraulic era will flourish and wishes them good luck for the future. *P. G. Barnes*

	Number	Name	Date Introduced	Date Withdrawn
Class 41	D600	*Active*	24/1/1958	30/12/1967
	D601	*Ark Royal*	28/3/1958	30/12/1967
	D602	*Bulldog*	3/11/1958	30/12/1967
	D603	*Conquest*	21/11/1958	30/12/1967
	D604	*Cossack*	20/1/1959	30/12/1967
Class 42	D800	*Sir Brian Robertson*	11/8/1958	5/10/1968
	D801	*Vanguard*	7/11/1958	3/8/1968
	D802	*Formidable*	16/12/1958	5/10/1968
	D803	*Albion*	16/3/1959	1/1/1972
	D804	*Avenger*	23/4/1959	3/10/1971
	D805	*Benbow*	13/5/1959	24/10/1972
	D806	*Cambrian*	3/6/1959	2/11/1972
	D807	*Caradoc*	24/6/1959	26/9/1972
	D808	*Centaur*	8/7/1959	3/10/1971
	D809	*Champion*	19/8/1959	3/10/1971
	D810	*Cockade*	16/9/1959	3/12/1972
	D811	*Daring*	14/10/1959	1/1/1972
	D812	*The Royal Naval Reserve 1859-1959 **	12/11/1959	3/11/1972
	D813	*Diadem*	9/12/1959	1/1/1972
	D814	*Dragon*	1/1/1960	7/11/1972
	D815	*Druid*	20/1/1960	3/10/1971
	D816	*Eclipse*	17/2/1960	1/1/1972
	D817	*Foxhound*	9/3/1960	3/10/1971
	D818	*Glory*	30/3/1960	1/11/1972
	D819	*Goliath*	25/4/1960	3/10/1971
	D820	*Grenville*	4/5/1960	2/11/1972
	D821	*Greyhound*	25/5/1960	3/12/1972
	D822	*Hercules*	15/6/1960	3/10/1971
	D823	*Hermes*	6/7/1960	3/10/1971
	D824	*Highflyer*	27/7/1960	3/12/1972
	D825	*Intrepid*	24/8/1960	23/8/1972
	D826	*Jupiter*	7/9/1960	18/10/1971
	D827	*Kelly*	4/10/1960	1/1/1972
	D828	*Magnificent*	19/10/1960	28/5/1971
	D829	*Magpie*	23/11/1960	26/8/1972
	D830	*Majestic ***	19/1/1961	26/3/1969
	D831	*Monarch*	11/1/1961	3/10/1971
	D832	*Onslaught*	8/2/1961	16/12/1972

Left:
After withdrawal the original A1A-A1A 'Warships' were stored at Laira until they were hauled to South Wales for breaking-up in July 1968. Nos D600 and D601 were sold to Woodham's, at Barry, and Nos D602-4 to Cashmore's, near Newport. All but No D603 had received works attention in 1967, but at the end of that year No D600 was in standard blue with full yellow ends, No D602 was also blue but with small panels and Nos D601/3/4 were still green with small panels. No D600 is seen at Laira on 16 August 1967 with the ugly route-indicator boxes that were eventually fitted to these locomotives. *C. H. S. Owen*

	Number	Name	Date Introduced	Date Withdrawn
Class 43	D833	*Panther*	6/7/1960	3/10/1971
	D834	*Pathfinder*	26/7/1960	3/10/1971
	D835	*Pegasus*	5/8/1960	3/10/1971
	D836	*Powerful*	13/9/1960	22/5/1971
	D837	*Ramillies*	8/11/1960	22/5/1971
	D838	*Rapid*	3/10/1960	27/3/1971
	D839	*Relentless*	12/11/1960	3/10/1971
	D840	*Resistance*	3/2/1961	26/4/1969
	D841	*Roebuck*	14/12/1960	3/10/1971
	D842	*Royal Oak*	20/12/1960	3/10/1971
	D843	*Sharpshooter*	2/1/1961	22/5/1971
	D844	*Spartan*	16/3/1961	3/10/1971
	D845	*Sprightly*	7/4/1961	3/10/1971
	D846	*Steadfast*	12/4/1961	22/5/1971
	D847	*Strongbow*	22/4/1961	27/3/1971
	D848	*Sultan*	27/4/1961	26/3/1969
	D849	*Superb*	29/5/1961	22/5/1971
	D850	*Swift*	8/6/1961	22/5/1971
	D851	*Temeraire*	10/7/1961	22/5/1971
	D852	*Tenacious*	24/7/1961	3/10/1971
	D853	*Thruster*	30/8/1961	3/10/1971
	D854	*Tiger*	26/9/1961	3/10/1971
	D855	*Triumph*	25/10/1961	3/10/1971
	D856	*Trojan*	16/11/1961	22/5/1971
	D857	*Undaunted*	11/12/1961	3/10/1971
	D858	*Valorous*	15/12/1961	3/10/1971
	D859	*Vanquisher*	9/1/1962	27/3/1971
	D860	*Victorious*	22/1/1962	27/3/1971
	D861	*Vigilant*	14/2/1962	3/10/1971
	D862	*Viking*	13/3/1962	3/10/1971
	D863	*Warrior*	7/4/1962	26/3/1969
	D864	*Zambesi*	10/5/1962	27/3/1971
	D865	*Zealous*	28/6/1962	22/5/1971
Class 42	D866	*Zebra*	24/3/1961	1/1/1972
	D867	*Zenith*	26/4/1961	8/10/1971
	D868	*Zephyr*	18/5/1961	3/10/1971
	D869	*Zest*	12/7/1961	3/10/1971
	D870	*Zulu*	25/10/1961	28/8/1971

*   *Originally allocated the name* Despatch

**   *Only Class 42 fitted with Paxman engines*

Class	Weight	Wheel arrangement	Engines	Power	Transmission	Speed
41	117 tons 8cwt	A1A-A1A	MAN	1,000hpx2	Voith	90mph
42	78 tons 12cwt	B-B	Maybach	1,135hpx2	Mekydro	90mph
(D800-2)	78 tons 12cwt	B-B	Maybach	1,035hpx2	Mekydro	90mph
(D830)	77 tons 16cwt	B-B	Paxman	1,135hpx2	Mekydro	90mph
43	80 tons 16cwt	B-B	MAN	1,100hpx2	Voith	90mph

Class	Fuel capacity	Wheel diameter	Length	Height	Boiler	Boiler-water capacity
41	800gal	43in	65ft	12ft 10in	Spanner	1,000gal
42	800gal	39½in	60ft	12ft 9½in	Spanner *	940gal
43	800gal	39½in	60ft	12ft 9½in	Stone-Vapor	940gal

* No D830 fitted with a Stone-Vapor train-heating boiler

Acknowledgements

Above:

No D603 *Conquest* was the least-photographed of the five original 'Warships'. This could have been attributable to its modest lifetime mileage of only 512,000 miles and to the lengthy periods it spent out of service awaiting spare parts. The locomotive was unique in being the only A1A-A1A 'Warship' not to be overhauled at Swindon during 1967. It is seen entering Plymouth North Road from the west in 1962. *Maurice Dart collection*

In the course of preparation of *The Power of the Warships* it has been necessary to call upon a number of friends, colleagues and acquaintants to contribute photographic and other material not only for the sake of completeness but also to improve the overall quality of the product. Indeed, rather unusually the work of more than 80 photographers has been included within the pages of this book, and sadly but inevitably, in view of the time scale covered by the photographs, many are no longer with us. In no particular order I should like to thank the following individuals and organisations for their help in a variety of ways. For photography I extend my sincere gratitude to Michael Mensing, Bryan Hicks, Peter Treloar, Geoff Gillham, Gavin Morrison, Colin Marsden, Maurice Dart, Phil Barnes, R. C. (Dick) Riley,

Dr John Cooper-Smith and the Stephenson Locomotive Society, in addition to all of the photographers whose names appear in the individual picture credits. For literary efforts I acknowledge the work of Brian Reed for *Diesel-Hydraulic Locomotives of the Western Region* (David & Charles, 1974) and Geoff Endacott for *'Westerns', 'Warships'* and *'Hymeks'* at Work (Ian Allan Publishing, 1988). Finally, I should like to thank Peter Waller and the production team at Ian Allan/OPC for their assistance and for the freedom afforded in terms of layout and design. The book is dedicated to all those preservationists who have toiled so hard and have spent so much of their hard-earned money to enable present and future generations to experience the sight and sound of a Maybach-engined 'Warship'.

Right:
Unbelievably No D601 *Ark Royal* slowly rotted in the Woodham's Yard sidings at Barry from 1968 until 1980 — longer than it had been in BR service! There were attempts to save the locomotive, but it lacked engines and other key components, and the cost of restoration would have been prohibitive. Thought was given to saving it merely as a body shell, but the required purchase price was too high. Thus, like the 'D63xx' (Class 22) 'Baby Warships' and the MAN-engined B-B (Class 43) 'Warships', these products of the now-defunct North British Locomotive Co are now, sadly, extinct. This photograph was taken at Barry in March 1973. *John Vaughan*